GOD'S
PHONE NUMBER

GOD'S PHONE NUMBER

Instantly Talk to God and Quickly Turn
Your Wishes Into Fulfilled Prayers

GOD'S PHONE NUMBER

Instantly Talk to God and Quickly Turn Your Wishes into Fulfilled Prayers

DANIEL ESSIEN

CONTENTS

CHAPTER 1

INTRODUCTION

This book is extremely powerful and life-changing. This book contains the secret to questions asked by the rich, the poor, the average, Christians, Muslims, the nonreligious, and people through millennia. It has changed my life. It has changed the lives of my friends, the lives of many other people, and it will change yours too, if you adopt the Principles in this book. I won't keep you in suspense for long. But first, let me tell you how this book came about, and then I promise that we will dive straight into the secret that you will cherish for the rest of your life.

While growing up, I tasted abject poverty along with my family. Nevertheless, I knew in my heart that I could become anything that I desired, even though I did not know how that could be possible. As a teenager and a young adult, I enjoyed learning in school and did extremely well. I thought to myself that: "If I could get all A's in my classes, I could become whatever I want to be." But I soon found out that this was only a partial truth. Even though I achieved many successes with my education, I realized that my education was not enough to achieve the life that I desired.

Within a short time after graduating from college, I reached the peak salary range in my industry, and my salary kept increasing annually. Yet, my increasing salary was not enough to satisfy or keep up with my growing desires. Consequently, after much thought, I decided to quit my job and start my own company. Unfortunately, at least from a superficial standpoint, my efforts to build my own company failed miserably. I then resorted to going to church to find comfort and answers. In church, I learned about faith, and I learned that if I had enough faith, I could achieve everything that I desired.

Unfortunately, that also did not work as I had expected. The type of faith I had learned was the kind of faith that presumed that: If a person works very hard, prays, and believes in God, then that person can achieve his or her dreams. This way of thinking turned out to be not entirely true, as I discovered that true faith does not require working very hard every day, especially to the point of daily physical and mental exhaustion. However, I achieved decent successes with this attitude and was able to birth a few successful businesses. Yet, I felt deep within me that something was missing. I also felt that I needed to do something different. So I started listening to other pastors on the TBN cable channel, especially Joel Osteen, who inspired me greatly.

In spite of all my efforts, I still had many unanswered questions. And I had a continuing desire to get my prayers fulfilled. Then I had a thought. It was not strong. It was more of a gentle feeling or a faint impulse. And with this impulse, I began to read about what it meant to communicate with God. I wanted to be able to talk to God anytime, like the way I do when I want to talk to a good friend. I wanted to be able to pick up the phone and call him anytime to learn *the secret method*—if there was one—to turn my unfulfilled wishes into fulfilled prayers. Perhaps, one could say that what I really wanted was *God's Phone Number*. For a long period of time, I kept searching for this "phone number," but I barely made progress in my pursuit. However, I did not give up. I wanted to make sure that God could hear me, and I could hear his responses as well.

Consequently, I went from one author to another, and I later read a book titled "Conversations with God" written by Neale Donald Walsh. This book challenged me to my core and provided answers to many of the questions I had sought answers for over the years. Then one day, I decided to write down some one-liner phrases of principles I had learned in my life and spiritual quest on my basement wall for myself and my family. It was supposed to be my family's ten commandments for life. I wanted to write them so that we would not forget to apply them. Examples of the one-liner phrases I wrote were "The Law of Least Effort" and "The Law of Detachment."

Soon I realized that not only was my basement wall not big enough to contain the phrases, but also, the phrases by themselves did not give detailed explanations of the principles for myself and for my family. Little did I know at the time, that I would soon receive directly from God detailed explanations that covered my phrases and many more subjects.

One night, sometime between 3 and 5 a.m. in the morning, I was awoken by something. I don't know what it was. I was lying in bed and could not fall back to sleep. Suddenly, I heard a voice speaking to me. I thought I was talking to myself. The voice said to **Me:**

How about you write a book about the principles you've been writing on your basement wall so that your children and posterity can benefit from it? I can help you. In fact, I already have the complete Table of Contents for the book. Not only will your posterity benefit from it, but the whole world will as well. Get up and write down the following Table of Contents, and I will lead you to write the book.

So I got up and wrote down the Table of Contents for the book. I thought I was dreaming, but I found out when I awoke in the morning that it was real. I was so excited about the book and talked to my wife about it in the morning. She was somewhat skeptical, but she was encouraging.

Then something mystical happened. Each time I

would start writing something related to the content of the book, the voice would take control and tell me what to write. And when I asked the voice a question in my mind, the voice would answer. Before I knew it, I had actually started a conversation with God. Sometimes, I would ask a question and the voice would tell me to wait and to focus on something else until I was really ready for the answer. Sometimes, the voice gave me words to write so fast that I would write down five to ten pages within a time span of an hour or two. At some point, this process of writing became very exhausting, as I would wake up at night to write and not get enough sleep. As a result, I struggled to stay awake during the day at work. I remember praying one night and asking God to please let me have a sound sleep, as I did not want to wake up in the middle of the night to write. Soon, however, I learned how to cooperate with the voice and manage my time. But even still, the voice continued to speak to me at many different times and places. The voice talked to me while in traffic, at my daughter's orchestra concert, in the middle of helping a customer at work, while I was quiet for just a couple seconds, while I was talking to my wife and during work meetings. It also talked to me while I was working out, at parking lots, while waiting for my food at a drive-thru, at the airport, inside an airplane and many more places. Basically, the voice talked to me everywhere and whenever it wanted to. Over time, the process of receiving and writing became my lifestyle and very comfortable. Some days, the voice spoke a lot, and other days, it only whispered one or two things. There were some days when I wanted the voice to give me information about a topic, but the voice would not respond. I soon learned that all I needed to do was to ask and simply wait until I was physically, mentally, and spiritually ready to receive the answer.

Initially, I thought it was my own mind that kept talking to me, so I doubted, and I still doubt sometimes. However, whenever I consider the depth of knowledge or insight with which the voice spoke to me and how the Principles I obtained have transformed my life, I give up all doubts.

On the first day that the voice gave me the Table of Contents for this book, I asked the voice to tell me who it was and it answered by saying: "I am God." I could not believe it, but I decided to play along and listen to all that the voice had to tell me. I later confirmed and got more assurances that I was not going crazy and that others have had similar experiences. Despite all the assurances, I sometimes struggle to accept messages from the voice, as the Principles that the voice utters generally go against my conventional way of thinking. I therefore take it one day at a time to apply the Principles in my life to help me decipher the sense and truth in them.

Just like Neal Donald Walsh, who has had a similar experience, and said that it just happened to him, this book also just happened to me within a period of three and a half months. I believe this book is inspired by God. However, please do not take my word for it. I ask that you simply be open-minded, and read this book in its entirety to decide if there is something in the conversation that you are about to read that can help you. If something is not helpful, please disregard it, and take only that which appeals to you.

It is my sincere hope that this book will challenge you and help you to begin your own conversation with God as well, as we all have access to God. I must admit that since this book was written, I have found myself having to reread it from time to time to make sure I am living the truths that it contains. So don't feel bad if you have to reread it as well to ensure full comprehension. I also do not claim to know on a mental or conscious level everything about prayer or God. However, as a long-lasting effect of writing this book, I have been trying to be the best person I can be on a daily basis. And I continue to press on to take hold of the Principles contained in this book, and the perfection that many great spiritual teachers have left at our disposal.

For this reason, I ask for forgiveness from all the people that I have offended in the past and may unknowingly offend in the future. I hope we can all work together to build a better future for all people. Likewise, I forgive all those who have offended me in the past and may offend me in the future.

With that said, you are only a few moments away from having a supernatural conversation with God through me, and soon through yourself. This book contains organized pieces of a conversation that I have had with God. It covers topics such as who God is, prayer, faith, meditation, manifestation, awareness, spiritual laws, etc. It will teach you how to pray to manifest your desires. It is important, however, to read this book in its entirety, from beginning to end, rather than skipping through the chapters. This will give you the best understanding, as each chapter builds on its preceding chapter. I am hopeful that you will enjoy it and reread it many times.

It is also worth mentioning that as a consequence of having this conversation, I became accustomed to the voice, and the voice assured me that it was okay to converse either formally or informally. So don't be surprised to see parts of this conversation switch from formal to informal and vice versa.

With that said, now is the moment that you have been waiting for – so without a second thought, take a deep breath, and let's call God's phone number to listen to what he has to say.

CHAPTER 2

THE MAKEUP OF GOD

This conversation begins with a question that I asked God....

Me: I have prayed all the prayers that I can pray and done all the fasting that I can do. Even though I am somewhat confident in you, for the most part, I feel like you may not be getting my messages.

Sometimes, I feel like you do receive my messages, but you simply decide to ignore me. Other times, I feel like some of my prayers may be unrighteous, or that you are not answering my prayers because of something bad that I did in the past. It gets frustrating, and it makes me feel that you might not even exist at all. Am I doing something wrong? Could you tell me how to pray to get my prayers answered?

God: I have been getting all your messages, and I have been answering every single one of them without exception.

Me: How? How come I still have lots of unanswered prayers?

God: Well, let us take some time to discuss what prayer is in order to make sure you understand what it means to pray to get your prayers answered. But before we get started with prayer, it is extremely important for you to know what God is made of or who God is. Once you know what I am made of, or who I am, you will be able to pray more effectively to get results. So let's talk about what I am made of, and then we will talk about prayer. Do you know what God is made of?

Me: Yes, God is a spirit.

God: You are correct. God is a spirit. Everything that you experience with your five senses is also a spirit. The difference between the spirit that you call God, and what you see or experience with your five senses, is how fast or how slow the spirit is moving or vibrating. The effect of a spirit in fast-motion or slow-motion is still a spirit in motion regardless, but I understand that you call a spirit in slow-motion *physical* and a spirit in fast-motion *spiritual*. If a spirit is moving slowly, you can experience it with your five senses, but if it is moving very fast, you will not even see it with your ordinary naked eyes when it passes by you. A spirit is simply a principle in action. For example, when you clap your two hands, you hear a sound. You hear the sound because of a principle that says that: When two elastic objects are struck together to cause a vibration, then the effect should be a sound that your ears can hear. This principle can be applied anywhere on your planet with any two elastic objects, and the result will always be a sound. In the above example, the effect of the principle is called a sound. The principle and its effect are the same because without the principle the effect will not exist and vice versa. The principle exists for the purpose of making sound, so the principle itself is sound.

Me: What does sound have to do with me praying to achieve my desire to live a joyful life? Should I go around making sounds all day in order to enjoy life?

God: I gave you that example because your understanding of principles and their effects will help you create anything that you desire. Principles themselves are God. In your Bible, it is stated that: *In the beginning was the Word, and the Word was with God, and the Word was God. It was through the Word that all things were created; without the Word, nothing was created that has been created* (John 1:1-3). The Word is the same as my Principles. So God is Principles or the Word in action. Everything that you experience is as a result of the application of a Principle or the Word. The correct application of the Principles that God is made up of will bring you joy, and the incorrect application will bring you sorrow.

Me: So you mean God is just Principles and not a being that is in heaven?

God: Well, God is everywhere, but keep in mind that the Principles that God is made up of are constantly in motion through their application.

Me: So how can I know and understand these Principles so I can apply them correctly?

God: Good question. These Principles are all around you. You can see them, touch them, feel them, hear them, smell them, feel them with your sixth sense, and even taste them.

Me: What??? So you mean that I am seeing, hearing, touching, smelling, and tasting God every day? I thought the Principles were in the Bible.

God: Yes, they are; however, there are more Principles that have not been written in the Bible or in any books that you currently have on your planet. This is because my Principles, or Word, has infinite applications that go way beyond the Bible. Yet, all of my Principles can be described by one word, called "Love." Take for example, the

Principles of gravity, thermodynamics, or the Pythagoras theorem. People in the Bible may have experienced these Principles, but the Principles themselves have not been written about in the Bible in a way that offers easy understanding.

Me: But those are scientific laws and not moral laws.

God: Well, I tell you that man shall not live by moral Principles alone, but by any other Principle that is beneficial and is an expression of love. All Principles are my Principles whether you call them moral or scientific. Your understanding of Principles will bring you what is popularly called enlightenment. The more understanding you get of Principles and how to correctly apply them, the more enlightened you will become. When you understand how a Principle works, you can choose to apply the Principle whenever and wherever you like. The good news is that you do not have to be aware of all of my Principles to start having a joyful life.

Also, remember that the Principle (Word) is God himself, and there is no difference between a Principle and its effect. In other words, there is no difference between the cause of something and the effect of the cause. The effect exists as a manifestation of the cause, and without the effect, the cause will not exist. Everything that exists does so because something caused it to exist, and that something is the Principle, or the Word, or God. What

I intend to show you in this dialogue is some of the causes, so that you can use the cause or God to have a joyful life, because God is the cause (the Word or the Principles) of everything. Before we talk about some of the Principles, it is very important for you to understand a subtle difference between Principles and their effects as well as the different categories of Principles.

Me: Okay, please go ahead.

God: First, your Bible states that everything that was created in the beginning was made by God, or the Principle, and without it (Word or God) was not anything that is made that was made. You also know that it is impossible for a dog to give birth to a human being and vice versa. Based on what I just said, it holds true that God cannot give birth to something that is not a form of God. This is why the Bible further states that God created man in his own image and likeness. And this further explains what I said earlier: That the Principle and its effect are one, because one cannot exist without the other. Therefore, humans cannot exist without God because humans are the effect and God is the Cause (Word), which means that humans are one with God.

Me: Wait a minute. If humans are one with God, then humans are essentially God. Is that correct?

God: Yes, you got it. This is why the Bible states that, "Ye are gods..." (Psalm 82:6), and Jesus said that "I and the Father are one" (John 10:30). This is because all causes and their effects are inseparable by law or by Principle or by the initial Word, which is God himself.

Me: Hmmm, that's interesting.

God: Put differently, God cannot separate himself from himself. It further holds true that it is impossible for anything that is made in the image and likeness of God to operate without the Principle that it was made of. In order for God to create, God first had to create using himself (Word or Principle), which means that the result of God's creation was a replica of himself. Which further suggests that God cannot create anything that is not in his image or likeness. This further suggests that in order to create anything, one must first BE the thing that one seeks to create. Therefore, for a person to become joyful, the person has to BE joyful (or be aware of the Principles that produce joy), and for a person to become a doctor, the person has to BE a doctor (or know the Principles that govern or produce the act of being a doctor). The interesting thing is that the Word that you are made up of is capable of creating anything you pray for, except that you are merely unaware of it.

Me: Oh wow! But wait, just to make sure I understand

what you are saying, even though you have said something similar before, let me ask you this: If God cannot create anything separate from himself, then does that mean that I am not separate from you? And if I am not separate from you, then does that mean that I am you?

God: Yes, you got it again.

Me: If I am you, then can you just go ahead and order everything that I desire to manifest now, so that I don't have to try hard to enjoy life? After all, there is nothing impossible for God, right?

God: Yes, there is nothing impossible for me to do, but the only thing that is impossible for me to do *is* to do something that is against myself or my Principles.

Me: And that is?

God: Remember I told you that I am Principles, and that I must follow my own Principles. I cannot follow a Principle that does not define me. I cannot pretend to be something that is not me. Let me explain further what my Principles are, and it will all become clear. My Principles are divided into three main categories. Once you understand the three types of Principles that I am made of, you will understand why I cannot do for you what you are asking me to do by myself, but I can do it through you if you allow me or cooperate with my Principles.

Me: I see.

God: Principles and their effects are like a coin with two sides. One side is called the Principle, and the other side is called the effect. The Principle that creates a joyful life is on one side of a coin, and the effect, which is a joyful life, is on the other side of the same coin. They are inseparable. Now that you know that Principles and the effects of Principles in action are merely two sides of a coin or the same thing, let me tell you about the different types of Principles.

There are three broad types of Principles. Many people call them conscious mind, subconscious mind, and superconscious mind. Others call them mind, body, and soul. Most Christians call them the Father, the Son, and the Holy Spirit; or the Trinity. Other Christians also call them spirit, soul, and body. For easy understanding, I will call them conscious mind, subconscious mind, and superconscious mind. Your understanding of these three categories and how they work will help you to pray effectively to receive answers to your prayers. The three Principles must operate in harmony in order to get the best result.

Me: Let me make sure I understand. Are you saying

that God, who is made up of Principles, is made up of conscious mind, subconscious mind, and superconscious mind?

God: Yes. All the Principles are grouped based on their function. The conscious mind is made up of Principles that are responsible for physical manifestation. Some people call this manifestation the body of God in action. The subconscious mind is made up of Principles that produce what you call the soul of God. The soul is simply responsible for giving life to what the conscious mind or body thinks. Even though the soul gives life, it does not have all the right Principles that will give the conscious mind the most enjoyable and fulfilling life, unless it obtains the Principles from the superconscious mind. The superconscious mind is responsible for giving all souls the best ways (Principles) to give an enjoyable life to their conscious minds (body). There is only one superconscious mind, and this mind is connected to all people. The superconscious mind can be seen as the ultimate wisdom of God. People who do not understand these categories usually refer to the superconscious mind as God, and they forget that the superconscious mind is directly connected to their subconscious and Conscious minds, and that the three are inseparable. In order for the conscious mind (body) to do anything, it must contact the subconscious (soul), which has access to the Wisdom of God for creation. If the body fails to contact the soul, then anything that the body does cannot be in the image of itself. This is because the body is directly connected to the soul and the superconscious. Therefore, the body cannot separate itself and say that it wants to create something in its own image. It can only create something that is in the image of itself, which is the Trinity (also known as conscious, subconscious, and superconscious minds). Anything that the body creates that is not in the image of the conscious (body), subconscious and superconscious minds is an illusion that lacks the wisdom of the superconscious mind. The superconscious mind, which is the wisdom of God, contains all the instructions on how to create a happy and joyful life. Some of the wisdom (Principles) of God are shown in the body and all creation, but there is a vast amount of wisdom that has not been tapped into by the body for its use. The conscious mind (or body) cannot create without the soul and the soul cannot create without the body. Likewise, the superconscious mind cannot create without the soul and the conscious mind. This is the law, this is the Principle, this is God, and this is how the Principles (or the different parts of God) function together. This is why I told you that I could not create anything for you without your cooperation.

Me: So how do I cooperate so you can create through me?

God: It's simple. You just have to understand the Principles that your body is made of, the Principles that your soul is made of, and the Principles that your superconscious is made of, so that you can let all the Principles work in harmony to create whatever you pray for or imagine.

Me: Okay. Tell me more about how I cooperate, but before you do that, can you tell me the relationship between the three types of Principles and the Holy Spirit? Is the Holy Spirit a fourth spirit in addition to the Conscious, Subconscious, and superconscious minds?

God: First of all, all spirits are holy. However, when people use the word Holy Spirit, without them knowing exactly what it is, what they are really referring to is the Wisdom/Word of the superconscious mind. Every time a person (body or conscious mind) contacts the subconscious mind for a particular wisdom, the subconscious mind in turn contacts the superconscious to receive that wisdom. Upon receiving the wisdom, the subconscious passes the wisdom to the conscious mind of the person. When this happens, the person or the conscious mind is considered to have received the Holy Spirit Baptism. Any person who receives the wisdom of the Holy Spirit, and applies that wisdom, is said to be enlightened. This is exactly what happened on the Pentecost day in the Bible when the Holy Spirit fell upon the disciples. Some of the wisdom of the superconscious mind was simply brought into the awareness of the disciples. Just so there is no confusion, whenever I mention the name Holy Spirit, please know that I am referring to the one superconscious mind that is the mind of all people.

Me: Oh, my Goodness! This makes so much sense. So the description of a fire-like spirit that fell on the heads of the disciples that we are taught in church is not quite accurate then.

God: Well, when the wisdom of the superconscious mind fell on the disciples, it did appear as fire for a purpose, but that wisdom, or the spirit, was not a fourth spirit separate from the Conscious, subconscious and superconscious minds of all people. The superconscious spirit or mind manifested itself differently. Remember that the Word is a spirit, and everything is a spirit, as stated previously. So yes, the disciples had a spirit fall on them, as stated in the Bible. This is the same thing that happens when a person receives Christ as their Lord and Savior. When a person accepts or receives Christ as their Lord and Savior, what they are really doing or saying, is that they are going to humble themselves (Conscious mind) to receive the wisdom of their own superconscious mind through their subconscious mind.

It is worth noting that in the past, many people thought they could only receive the Holy Spirit (superconscious wisdom) through a priest. However, after the death of Jesus Christ, it became clear that all people have access to the Holy Spirit (superconscious mind), either through a priest, or through one's own subconscious mind, or through anybody that is an embodiment of the Holy Spirit.

Do you remember when Jesus said that the Holy Spirit, whom the Father will send as his representative, will teach and remind you of all things (John 14:26)? What he actually meant was that the Father was going to allow the manifold wisdom of God (superconscious mind) to fall on all people, either through their subconscious minds, or through priests, or through all that are embodiments of the Holy Spirit.

Consequently, anyone who receives the Holy Spirit can teach and remind others of the Father (wisdom of the superconscious mind). This explains why after the death of Christ, people became aware that anybody who has the wisdom of the Father (Holy Spirit) is a priest and can perform the function of a priest. Furthermore, this explains the tearing of the curtain in the New Testament – that all people (Conscious minds) can access the one superconscious mind through themselves, or through others that are operating in harmony with their Subconscious and superconscious minds. Therefore, do not only perceive the Holy Spirit as some invisible being, as the Holy Spirit has entered many people, and the people have become embodiments of the Holy Spirit. These people are some of the great pastors, sages, priests, and teachers you see and hear today. But, be careful of their messages, because not everyone who says the name of the Father (superconscious mind) is really preaching a beneficial application of the wisdom of the Father. To be careful and to be able to decipher what is beneficial, study this book, the Bible and other great sources of my Word.

Here is another way to understand this. Any soul that *is* birthed in human form to teach and remind people of the Holy Spirit is the Holy Spirit. Often, such people have evolved in their current life or previous lifetimes by gaining a deeper understanding of knowledge that they have received from their superconscious mind.

The Holy Spirit is not another spirit that is separate from the spirit that already lives in all men. Rather, it is simply the wisdom (Word) of the superconscious mind. It will not surprise you to know that some scientists and people from various religions are not recognized as being spiritual or religious by everyone. However, such people are also embodiments of the Holy Spirit. This is because they have also downloaded information from the one superconscious mind into their subconscious minds, and subsequently into their conscious minds. So the Holy Spirit is not only in churches. In fact, all people are to some extent an embodiment of the Holy Spirit. This is because all people have different degrees of conscious awareness of the Holy Spirit that resides in them. The lower the consciousness of the Holy Spirit that a person has, the more it will seem that the person does not have the Holy Spirit – which, in fact, is not entirely accurate.

Me: So how do I tap into this wisdom or Word, or the Holy Spirit, or my superconscious mind in order to create a joyful life?

God: Did you hear yourself? You just said the Word, wisdom, or the Holy Spirit, or my superconscious mind. That means you are paying attention.

Me: Oh yes, I am paying attention. Who wouldn't pay attention when talking to God?

God: You would be surprised how many people do not. I talk to all people every day, but only a few actually listen. In fact, you just started paying a little closer attention to my voice recently. Do you know how long I have been trying to get your attention?

Me: How long?

God: A very very long time. Longer than you can think of with your present consciousness or understanding.

Me: Interesting.

God: In order to tap into the wisdom of the Holy Spirit, you first have to download information or Principles from the Holy Spirit. The downloading of the Principles is done through **prayer. You can initiate the download of**

information from your superconscious mind by making a request for your fulfilled desires through prayer.

Notice I said that you could request for your <u>fulfilled</u> desires and not your desires. This is because your desires have already been fulfilled, but you just don't know it yet. My Principles do not exist in a vacuum. They exist for the purpose of solving problems. So, whenever you have a need or desire, ask me for the Principles associated with your need through prayer and I will answer. In fact, even before you ask, I would have already answered, but your asking will initiate your exposure to the answers or Principles I have already provided.

Me: So how long do I have to pray to tap into this wisdom? Not only do I pray, but I have been fasting too. How come I have not been able to tap into my superconscious mind?

God: I know. You have been praying all your life, and I have been answering all your prayers. There is not a single prayer that you have ever prayed that I have not answered.

Me: What do you mean? Have you really answered all my prayers? And if that is the case, why can't I see it? Are you saying that you answer every prayer everybody prays? I was told that you sometimes do not answer our prayers because we sometimes do not know what is good for us.

God: I do answer all your prayers whether they are good or bad.

Me: Hold up! You answer bad prayers too? I was told that God only answers one's prayer when the prayer is aligned with God's will. So how do you answer bad prayers? And if you answer all prayers, how come you have not answered my prayer for a nice house?

God: First, understand that I cannot withhold anything from you, whether good or bad, because whatever you desire in your conscious mind, your subconscious mind has no choice but to manifest it. This is a universal Principle, this is my Word, and this is a law. However, note that the speed at which your prayers will get answered will be so much faster when the thing that you are praying for is to be used to express pure love. This is because it takes your conscious mind, your subconscious mind, and your superconscious mind to bring into existence anything that you pray for that expresses pure love. Whereas it takes only your conscious mind and subconscious mind to bring into existence anything that you pray for that is not an expression of pure love. Three is better than two. The power of three is not just one more than two, but it's a zillion times greater, as your superconscious contains all the wisdom of God. Also, I have already answered all your prayers, but the question is: Did you pay attention when you were prompted on how you can get your nice house? It may be a little confusing for now, but let's talk a little bit, and you will begin to understand and know that I have already answered all of your prayers whether your prayers were good or bad.

Me: Okay, but you just brought in the subject of pure love. So before you go on, can you explain what pure love is?

God: Sure. Pure love is a Principle that manifests itself, without any force outside itself, through giving to itself or another, either for the mere joy of giving or for an exchange. From a physical standpoint, pure love either gives to itself or to another; but from a spiritual standpoint, pure love always gives to itself because there is no other person in the spiritual realm, as everything and everyone is interconnected and thereby one. Pure love, therefore, is simply giving without any intention of harming or taking advantage of another in the physical plane. Do you understand what pure love is now?

Me: Yes, I do. That's a great explanation. I never thought about it that way.

God: Now you know what pure love is, and the three

broad categories of Principles that you and I are made up of. So, let us discuss what prayer is - the five stages of prayer, and the Principles that govern each stage. Afterward, we will discuss how you can use the various stages along with faith to create and to BE anything that you imagine or pray for.

CHAPTER 3

WHAT IS PRAYER?

Me: What is prayer?

God: Prayer is simply a conversation with God. The act of praying can be equated to the act of playing hide and seek. When two children, namely child A and child B, are playing hide and seek, child B runs far away from child A, and child A is then supposed to find child B. Why would child A let child B run from his sight and then look for child B that was just in his sight? The answer is that the act of searching and the feeling of being searched for produces a nice thrill for both children. However, when child A gets tired of playing the hide and seek game, all child A has to do is to call out the name of child B and say that I am tired of playing the game, and that child B should come out of his or her hiding place, and then child B will indeed stop hiding and come to child A. This is not magic. That is the same thing that happens with prayer. You already have everything that you pray for. But you have hidden them from your own sight so that you can try to find them to get a thrill. If you understand this truth, then you will know that you already have everything, and you are merely pretending not to have it so you can find it again. Your soul knows this truth, and so does your Superconscious. When you are bored or tired of looking for something that you already have, all you have to do is to call forth the name of what you already have, and it will appear just like child A has to call the name of child B for child B to show up. This is why the Bible says, ...*let the weak say I am strong* (Joel 3:10). This is because the weak person is merely pretending to be weak so he or she can find his or her own strength again; otherwise, there will be nothing for the person to find or do. If therefore, you feel that you are tired of playing the game, all that you have to do is to stop playing and start praying to bring forth all that belongs to you. When the poor say that they are rich or the weak say that they are strong, they are not just pretending or merely stating some nice affirmations, but they are indeed stating a fact. This is why some people say that you need to fake it till you make it, but I tell you what, it is not necessary to fake it because you are it already, so *be* it, and sooner than later your conscious mind and the whole world will attest to the truth that your soul and superconscious mind already know. However, if you feel that it is hard to *be* something without physically seeing it, then I will suggest that you start by pretending to *be* it, so as to temporarily bypass your logical mind, and over time, you will gather enough conviction to *be* it and *become* it.

Me: So you mean I can call forth whatever I want, and it shall come to me?

God: Yes, but before your prayer is physically answered, you must first prepare a meal (food) for your subconscious mind. Everybody needs food for their physical bodies in order to live. Everybody also needs some pleasure, such as playing football or dancing, to enjoy the process of life. In the same way, every soul or subconscious mind needs food and pleasure to experience an enjoyable life. If you fail to give your subconscious mind food to eat, you will prevent its growth, or you will slow its vibration(movement) and thereby slow down the life that it gives to your body. Remember that your subconscious mind is a Word or Principle in action. The action that the Principle is performing can be slowed down by you if you do not give it the food that it desires.

The most desirable food for all souls is a good prayer. In order for the food for the soul to be well prepared it must go through five stages of cooking. Trust me that this process is not long. Once you master it, you can prepare a good meal (food) in seconds for your subconscious mind. The fact that your prayer, which is food, is well prepared does not mean that your prayer is the best one for your soul. It is the same as saying that the fact that junk food is well prepared does not mean that it has all the right ingredients. A perfect prayer or food for the soul has all the right ingredients for growth, nourishment, and pleasure. A perfect prayer also produces a ripple effect of benefiting other souls without causing any physical or psychological harm to another. According to the Bible, God desires that you prosper and have a good future (Jeremiah 29:11). When a person feeds his or her soul with the right food, the person is doing the will of God and thereby prospering the soul. When a soul is prosperous, the conscious mind or body prospers as well in all areas.

Me: Where do I get the right ingredients to prepare good food for my soul or my subconscious?

God: All the ingredients for good food are already available to you. What you have to do is to pick the appropriate ingredients that you can use to prepare the best food for your soul. You pick the ingredients by simply choosing what kind of thoughts you want to have. Some thoughts produce good health, and other thoughts produce bad health. For example, if you believe that a particular life activity such as smoking is bad for you, yet you keep thinking about smoking, that means you are picking the wrong ingredient (thought) to prepare a good meal (food) for your soul. This is because if you continue to have the thought of smoking, your subconscious will take that thought of smoking as your prayers and manifest it by making you smoke. Two or more thoughts held by faith produces food for the soul. So your thoughts make up your prayers. Your thoughts must go through five stages to produce a meal (or food) for your soul. The stages are: Ordinary thought, wish, desire, passion, and awareness. With that said, let us look at each stage of prayer.

The Five Stages of Prayer (The Makeup of Prayer)

Stage 1: Ordinary Thought/Image

A thought is simply your judgment or feeling or idea about something. An ordinary thought is a thought that is not repeated often in your mind. For example, if I ask you: *"Do you think you will ever have $50,000 in your bank account?"* And you say something like: *"Hmmm... I don't think so. I don't know how I can get that kind of money."* The question I put forth is an ordinary thought that your mind processes and the answer that you give is also an ordinary thought that your mind produces. Likewise, if you asked yourself the same question and you answered yourself, then you would have had two ordinary thoughts. The next stages of prayer will explain how your ordinary thoughts get transformed into other stages of prayer. Anytime you think about something, you produce one or more thoughts and your thoughts create your feelings. Your feelings in turn cause you to have further thoughts and your further thoughts cause you to have new feelings, and the cycle goes on until you change your thoughts. Every ordinary thought that you have is a prayer, whether good or bad. Each ordinary thought or prayer you produce is immediately received by your subconscious and superconscious minds. This is the first stage of prayer. Since all thoughts are prayers in themselves, you do not necessarily have to kneel down solemnly to pray because every ordinary thought that you have is transmitted to both your subconscious mind (soul) and your superconscious mind (Father in Heaven) regardless of which position you are in.

Me: Is there something wrong with solemnly kneeling down to pray?

God: There is nothing wrong with that or any traditional or ritualistic style of prayer you can think about. The point I am trying to make is that you can pray whether you are kneeling down, singing, eating, etc. Most masters pray more fervently while doing their daily routine activities than they do when praying in a ritualistic way God looks at your heart more than your position, but if you have to express what is on your heart by kneeling or by having any other posture, that is perfectly fine with me. Most masters generally pray ritualistically or solemnly to set an example for young believers to follow, as that helps young believers to establish some respect, seriousness, and a routine for praying. They also do it to help others to tap into the collective energy of a group. This again does not mean it is wrong to pray in a ritualistic form. However, when you understand what prayer is, and the general purpose for ritualistic prayers, then you can be at ease to pray in any setting. Prayers offered in different settings will meet the same or similar objectives that ritualistic prayers are intended for. But if you prefer, you can keep your ritualistic prayers and pray in other settings as well to augment and enhance your ritualistic prayers.

Me: That makes sense.

God: I stated that every ordinary thought that you have is transmitted to both your subconscious mind (soul) and your superconscious mind (Father in heaven). You can confirm what I am telling you by reading Jeremiah 17:10, which states that: I the Lord (superconscious) search the heart (subconscious) and examine the mind (conscious mind), to reward each person according to their conduct, according to what their deeds deserve. Your conduct includes the things that you think about because every thought (or thinking) is an act of doing something and therefore a deed. This is why a lot of research has been done to prove the power of thoughts. You can check out books like "The Power of Your Subconscious Mind" and

"The Intention Experiment" that will confirm to you the power of your thought. A thought can have the effect of healing, joy, raising the dead, causing many miracles, causing many diseases, etc. Therefore, make sure that every thought that you have relates directly to what you desire and not what you do not desire, as it can have very large effects. Also make sure you always think well of others as you would think of yourself because if you think negative about others, the negative thought will first affect you before it affects the person you intended the thought for. This is because of the universal Principle (Word or God) that we discussed earlier that... you cannot give birth to something that is not in your own image. If you have any unkind thoughts about anything or anybody, you first have to be the thing that you are thinking about before your thought can have an effect on another. Let me explain this a little further, as it is very important, and it has so much to do with how happy or sorrowful you can become. There are five main categories of ordinary thoughts. The first type of ordinary thoughts are the thoughts that you think about yourself, and the second type of ordinary thoughts are the thoughts that you think about others. The third type of ordinary thoughts are the thoughts that you think about your business (family, job or establishment), and the fourth type of ordinary thoughts are the thoughts that you think about others' businesses (family, job or establishment). The fifth type of ordinary thoughts are the thoughts that you have about nonhumans or other objects that exist in the universe.

Make sure not to think any negative thought about others and their business or family, as whatever you think of them you will first become. For example, do not think that another person is crazy, stupid, weird, greedy, etc., even if they appear to be. There is a reason they appear to be the way you see them. So rather than seeing them in a negative light, you can decide to see them as young students who are learning as all of you are on different levels of learning or remembering. If you think that others that are below you in terms of evolution are stupid, then someone that is below or above you in terms of evolution may also think of you as stupid.

Imagine that you encounter a person who appears to be greedy. If you imagine that the person is generous, and you demonstrate generosity to this person over a period of time, then that person will eventually demonstrate generosity back to you. This is what God, or the Principles, or the Word, is all about. Jesus taught this by saying, *Do unto others what you want others to do unto you.* Buddha also taught this by saying: *Be the light you want to see in the world.* And Jesus also said that: "For in the same way you judge others, you will be judged, and with the measure you use, it will be measured to you" (Matthew 7:2). And Paul also wrote that: "Finally, brothers and sisters, whatever is true, whatever is noble, whatever is right, whatever is pure, whatever is lovely, whatever is admirable - if anything is excellent or praiseworthy - think about such things." (Philippians 4:8). You should see how powerful your thoughts are. In order for your ordinary thoughts to be effectively harnessed, you must take your thoughts through the second stage of prayer which is a "wish." Before we talk about your wishes, let me ask you a question. If I gave you the option to choose between $500.00 and $1,000.00, which one would you choose?

Me: I would choose the $1,000.00

God: Okay, so you chose the $1,000.00 obviously because it is more. Now, I'm sure that if I asked you to choose between the things you see and the things you don't see, you would probably choose the things that you see. But I tell you this: The things that you do not see are far bigger than the things that you do see. So it will be very good for you to choose more of the things that you do not see because the things that you do not see are the source of all that you do see. Therefore, make sure to focus your thoughts on things that you do not see (source or cause) that correspond more with your fulfilled desire than focusing your thought on things that you do see that are very limited. This will all become clearer to you by the time we are done going through this book. But for now, let's look at the second stage of prayer, which is a "wish."

Stage 2: Wish

A wish is an ordinary thought that you have every once in a while. Whenever you have a *wishful* thought, you generally change your thought to something else because you do not believe you can have what you wish for. It is also a thought about something that you think it will be nice to have, but you do not want it so bad. For example, you may wish you were able to travel across the world and not care if you do or don't. Or you may wish you had a billion dollars and not care if you do or don't get it.

An ordinary thought becomes a wish if it is repeated every once in a while. A wish is different from an ordinary thought in the sense that when you have a wishful thought, you generally imagine yourself having and using the thing that you wish for, except that *this* type of imagination only lasts for a brief moment. When you dwell on your wishes a little longer, by repeatedly imagining having your wish come true over time, your wish will then become a desire. Desire, therefore, is the third stage of prayer.

Stage 3: Desire

A desire is a wish that has been amplified a little bit over time through repeated imagining of the feeling that would be attained when the wish is fulfilled. A desire is a very strong wish. Many people do not move their ordinary thoughts to this stage because they do not think they can get what they wish for.

Desire is the food of the soul (subconscious). Whenever you have a desire, your soul jumps up and down in excitement because it knows it has food. When a man finds a woman that he loves and adores, he gets so excited and happy. The feeling that a soul gets from finding food (or desire) is like the feeling that a man gets when he meets the woman of his dreams, and he is so excited. The act of a person pondering over his desire over and over is like a man having intercourse with his wife. As the intercourse (the act of pondering over the desire) between the man (conscious mind) and the woman (soul or subconscious) grows or increases over a period of time, the man (conscious mind) releases a sperm (desire) into the woman's womb (subconscious mind) for fertilization. Once the desire is in the woman's or subconscious' womb, the desire turns into a zygote or passion. Passion is the next stage of prayer that we will be discussing. Once you have a passion or a zygote, it must be nurtured and fed by the subconscious – or the woman – in order to develop into a full being (manifestation of the desire). Failure to move a desire to a passionate stage is a denial of oneself, since the denial is against what the soul yearns for. The soul yearns to have intercourse with the conscious mind so that it can keep bringing forth a baby. Therefore, it is a sin against yourself to deny yourself of that which you deeply desire (passion).

It is very crucial to know that the only way to move your prayer from the stage of desire to the next stage, which is passion, is to have faith. Faith is simply believing that you can have what you desire. Faith requires that you not only believe in yourself, but also believe that all things will always work together for your good. This is true even when your present reality is the opposite of what you desire. We can discuss what faith is after we go through the five stages of prayer, but remember that faith is like a vehicle that is used to transport your desire to the next two stages of prayer, which are passion and awareness.

Stage 4: Passion

A passion is a desire that is imagined over and over such that the desire becomes an obsession. When your subconscious is pregnant with the little zygote or passion, it goes through a process of pregnancy to give birth to a child called awareness or consciousness. Your conscious mind (the man) must work to put food on the table for the subconscious mind (the woman) to eat to nourish the zygote or passion. Otherwise, the zygote will die. This work is done by exercising your faith. Note that your current thought is your current level of awareness and it is your current level of awareness that gets transformed into a passion and then eventually into a new awareness. Notice that awareness gives birth to a higher awareness. Whenever your soul is pregnant with a new passion, it is very common to notice yourself talking about your soon-to-be-born child (awareness) to your significant other (soul and Superconscious) verbally and non-verbally. Verbal communication is done through prayer (affirmations, songs, praying with words, etc.). Nonverbal communication is also done at this stage through constantly fixating one's mind on the new baby to be born. The new baby to be born will be a new awareness, or Principle/Word, or the Word in action (fulfilled passion).

To summarize, passion gives birth to awareness. Awareness is God himself. Awareness is the same as the Word of God. The Word of God is God himself. It is through the Word of God (awareness or nothingness or void) that something can be created. It is worthwhile noting that no one can manifest things in the physical realm that they don't have an awareness of. That is against the law of God. God cannot be something that is not God. Awareness cannot manifest itself into something that it is not aware of. In other words, it is impossible for a human being to give birth to a dog and vice versa. This explains why people who are gifted with inheritances, or people who win the lottery without having first gain the Principles associated with their gifts, end up losing what they have. They lose it because they are not aware of the awareness that produced what they have been given. The only way for such people to keep what they have is for them to find a capable and honest person – one who has a higher or equal awareness of what they have – to manage it for them.

Here is a big secret: At any given time, you have different prayers that are at different stages: Ordinary thoughts, wishes, desires, and passions. From a spiritual standpoint, all your prayers are answered instantaneously. However, from a physical or manifestation standpoint, God mostly answers your prayers by first rewarding your passionate thoughts, then your desires, then your wishes, and then your ordinary thoughts.

As a new learner of the act of prayer, it may take you some time to move your ordinary thoughts to a passion. However, as you become more experienced in the art of prayer, you will quickly learn how to instantaneously move your ordinary thoughts to a passion and thereby rendering the result of your prayers faster.

Me: But why do you wait for our prayers to get to the stage of passion before you answer us?

God: Imagine what could happen if I immediately fulfilled a thought that somebody had about killing someone when the thought was not intentional. Or imagine what would happen if I immediately fulfilled a thought about robbing a bank when the thought was not intentional. Or imagine what would happen if I immediately fulfilled a thought about being a millionaire. Or imagine the consequences of me granting a million dollars to a child as soon as the child thought about a million dollars. The child would not know what to do with the million, and the child would not have an opportunity to learn the Principles or Word associated with being a millionaire. Besides, the million may have very undesirable effects on the child. In all the cases above, imagine what the repercussions could be.

Me: I see. So you want me to be an embodiment of the Principle or Word before you give me the effect of the Principle or Word.

God: Yes, you got it. Now, note that just for the simple fact that the child thought about being a millionaire, I will still do something for the child.

Me: What will you do for the child?

God: I will immediately make arrangements for the child to learn my Principles about being a millionaire, but it's up to the child to decide whether to take the opportunity or not.

Me: Are you saying that you will do something for a child for merely having a thought that is not even a wish? If so, then why is it necessary for me to repeat my thoughts over and over for my prayers to get to the stage of passion, in order for me to receive answers to my prayers?

God: Whether you are a child or not, I do something for you when you have a thought. I make arrangements to encourage you to repeat your thought, so that your thought can get to the stage of passion and eventually to awareness. I do this by bringing you circumstances and situations that will encourage you to have thoughts that are similar to your original thought through the law of attraction. The more your thoughts are repeated, the more likely you will ask yourself questions related to your thoughts. Doing so will eventually bring you the awareness that you need to manifest what you are praying for. Each thought is very big and powerful and generally needs to be broken down through the process of repeated thought or re-imagination for easy execution. Let me give you this analogy. When you eat a piece of bread, you do not just swallow it instantly. But you start by continuously chewing on the bread to break it down into smaller pieces that you can swallow. A well-chewed food is easier for your body to absorb. If the bread is not chewed well, your body cannot easily digest it, and you may end up excreting the undigested bread. In fact, you may even have constipation. The same thing happens with your thoughts. Each thought that you have is very powerful, and it is so big that it can cause you to have mental constipation with symptoms of anxiety, frustration, suffering, pain, headache, etcetera, if it is not properly chewed on, or well-imagined and reimagined.

Me: Wait a minute, are you saying that there is a proper way to chew on thought and an improper way to chew on thought?

God: Yes.

Me: What is the difference?

God: The proper way to chew on your thought is to think or imagine and re-imagine only what you desire instead of what you do not desire. And it is believing that what you desire has already been made manifest even though you cannot physically see it yet. It also means you must continuously re-imagine what you will do with the outcome of your thoughts, rather than getting fixated and bogged down on how difficult it will be for your thought to bring you your desires. If you ask me for bread and I give it to you, I am sure the next thing you will do is to eat the bread. Correct? So if you believe that I have given you your daily bread, then do not waste time trying to figure out how you are going to get the bread that is already in your hand. But rather, use your time to imagine what it will feel like to eat or share the bread. For it is only after you have passionately enjoyed the feeling of having your prayer fulfilled that your conscious mind will be at ease to receive or figure out the awareness or answer that you desire.

Me: I see.

God: Also, know that your subconscious mind absorbs everything – all thoughts. However, some thoughts are easier to absorb and execute than others. If your subconscious mind or soul absorbs something that is too big and undefined, it generally spits it right back out. It is important to chew on your thoughts through a process of focused re-imagination to ensure that your thoughts are broken down enough for easy absorption and execution. Once you chew on your thoughts through re-imagination and focus, you will notice that your thoughts will then be broken down into sub-thoughts that your subconscious mind can easily absorb. For example, if you suddenly think about being rich, you have to keep re-imagining what it will be like to be rich. **This means that you have to think about other thoughts that are related to being rich.** For instance, how much money do you desire to have? What would you do with your riches? How would you feel about your riches? Etc., etc. All these are sub-thoughts of the initial thought of being rich. **The more you experience the fulfillment of your sub-thoughts through repeated thoughts and images in your mind, the easier it will be for your subconscious mind to absorb and execute your sub-thoughts. Each**

sub-thought carries its own energy. The combination of two or more sub-thought energies is what produces the force for executing any work. You cannot accomplish anything significant without the force produced by your sub-thoughts. Therefore, do anything that you can each day to generate this force and immerse yourself in it as much as possible. This force has been called "the alpha and the omega," or "the beginning and the end," down through the ages. This force goes into the future to gather energy by taking a snap-shot of the future. Then, it returns to the present to create the future, one step after the other, with the energy it has gathered. You will be pleased to know that this force can also travel into the past to gather energy for creation in the present. It does so by remembering a past accomplishment and the sub-thoughts that were related to that accomplishment.

Don't get me wrong. This force does encounter many challenges and obstacles. However, the more you generate this force, the greater the energy, wisdom, and awareness you will also generate to overcome all obstacles. This process does not happen overnight. If you consistently experiment with this force for even three to six months, and then look back at where you started from, you will be amazed by your new awareness and where it has taken you.

It is very important to think about how your thoughts are going to bring into existence what you desire. However, try not to think too much about how it is going to be done. But rather, imagine that your energized sub-thoughts have gone out into the world and brought back your fulfilled desire. And also, imagine what you will do with your fulfilled desire and how it makes you feel. This is because your subconscious knows exactly how to digest every single sub-thought as food, and then bring forth all the awareness or knowledge necessary for you to accomplish the desire that you have sub-thoughts about.

Me: So how do I know that I have chewed on my thought well enough for my subconscious to easily absorb and execute?

God: You will know that you have chewed well enough on your thought when your thought produces emotions or feelings that you desire. For example, if you want to be a TV star, think about what it will mean for you. Imagine *what it will feel like* to be on TV with all your fans talking very positively about you. Once you start feeling what it will be like for you to be a TV star, rest assured that your subconscious will definitely pick up your thoughts and place them on its priority list.

Me: So when I have chewed well on my thoughts; and I can feel my thoughts, and my subconscious has picked my intention or thoughts, then do I stop re-imagining the same thoughts and start imagining different thoughts?

God: To answer this question, let me ask you a question. What do you do when you eat a delicious meal that is not enough to get you full or satisfied? Would you request more of the same meal or request a different meal?

Me: I would request more of the same meal that I previously enjoyed.

God: The same thing happens with your thoughts. Once you re-imagine your thoughts over and over for your thoughts to produce some feelings, then you can stop at some point. But if the feelings you experienced were so good, then definitely make sure to re-imagine the same thoughts again. And generate the same feelings again and again, as often as you can, until you can physically see your thoughts manifested. For doing so will definitely speed up the manifestation of your thoughts.

Me: So let me make sure that I got this right. Are you saying that my prayers can be easily manifested if I repeat my thoughts or prayers over and over while generating the feelings associated with my fulfilled prayers?

God: Yes. But it is also extremely important to understand two more things that will help you to quickly move your thoughts to the stage of passion.

Me: What are these two things? I am eager to know! Please tell me!

God: You know it is said that good things come to those who wait, but I tell you that good things come to those who *act on my Principles*. Your action is a core indication of your faith. The two things are faith and a basic understanding of the order-of-operations in the spiritual realm. We will discuss both in detail, but for now, know that *faith is action*. Good things come to those who act by faith. Faith applied correctly can move your thoughts or prayers quickly from a thought form to awareness, and then to manifestation.

Me: I thought this was going to be simple, but it keeps getting complicated. You keep introducing different topics.

God: No, it is not complicated. It's the same topic. If you think it is complicated, it will be complicated. But if you think it's not, then it will be easy. In fact, you can master these concepts within a very short time. You can master them in a matter of weeks if you pay attention. And once you master these Principles, you will not even have to think about them to apply them – the Principles will be automatically applied for you.

Me: Okay, tell me how I can use faith to move my ordinary thoughts quickly to become a passion and then awareness.

God: Sure, but remember that we have been talking about the five stages of prayer, which are ordinary thoughts, wishes, desire, passion, and awareness. We have barely scraped the surface of awareness. Therefore, let me explain what awareness is, and then we will move quickly to discuss how your understanding of faith and spiritual order-of-operations will give you the basic, yet the advanced knowledge that you need to start praying effectively. Remember that I said, when your subconscious is pregnant with passion, it goes through a process of pregnancy to give birth to a child called awareness. Awareness is simply what God gives you as an answer to your prayers. So let's discuss awareness a little further.

Me: I have been trusting you all this time, but I'm beginning to get frustrated with the many things that I have to learn in order to simply ask God to give me something through prayer. I don't think that even my science 101 class was this hard.

God: So when you think about the process of asking God for something, how easy do you want it to be?

Me: I want it to be as easy as me saying abracadabra, and all that I am thinking about will appear before me.

God: Hmmm.... Well, you know, that will be like rocket science or impossible for God to do for you without you first understanding the concepts we are discussing. The good news is that if you continue to trust me for us to finish with this subject, you will not even have to say "abracadabra" for your prayers to be answered. You will just have to imagine your fulfilled prayers, and it will be done!

Me: Okay.

God: So let's talk about awareness.

Stage 5: Awareness/The Word/Principle

God: Awareness is simply your knowing of causes and effects, and your ability to invoke the correct cause to produce the desired effect. In other words, it is having the correct knowledge of many causes and their effects, and then applying the most appropriate cause for the desired effect.

Me: What kind of knowledge are you talking about?

God: Awareness is the same as the Principles that God is made up of. It is the original Word that was used to form the entire universe. Awareness is simply God. When you know the Principles that I am made up of, you can use them to create anything that you desire. When you pray, I give you my awareness so you can use it to manifest what you desire. In other words, because everything is made up of God, God cannot give you something that is outside himself, as that something does not exist. God, therefore, gives you himself as an answer to your prayer. Occasionally, however, God gives you exactly what you ask for, as opposed to giving you an awareness. For God to give you exactly what you ask for is for God to give you himself in a transformed manner. And for God to give you his awareness is for God to give you his pure or raw self, which is pure awareness. Put differently, God sometimes gives you the effect versus the cause. Whenever God answers your prayer by giving you an awareness, or a cause, or a Principle, then you have to understand the awareness to some extent, so you can use it to produce the desired effect. Awareness of any subject or a particular prayer contains all that is needed for the awareness to manifest itself. Awareness contains understanding, self-organizing power (strength/energy), creativity, knowledge, harmony, balance, joy, bliss, and many more attributes.

There are seven levels of awareness relative to the answering of your prayers that are important for you to know. But before we discuss that, let me explain awareness from a different angle.

Awareness is the reuniting of a person's conscious mind with his or her subconscious and superconscious minds. Awareness is the point where the conscious mind obtains the knowing or causes or Principles that the subconscious and superconscious have that ultimately leads to love. Awareness ensures that there is an equilibrium of Principles or causes on the conscious level, subconscious level, and superconscious level relative to what a person does. Awareness is generally called "enlightenment" in the East, but it is also called "self-actualization" or "self transcendence" in the West. The only way to obtain awareness is to pray fervently for it. When one gains awareness, one gains Principles that are the same at the conscious, subconscious and superconscious levels. At this stage, it is not just a combination or alignment of the conscious mind, subconscious mind, and superconscious mind, but rather, the impact of the three minds or Principles is bigger than the sum of the effects of the three minds. The effect of the three minds or Principles is what the Bible refers to as: "... God is able to do exceedingly above all things we can ask or think or imagine..." (Ephesians 3:20). This is because God, or superconscious, knows what you need better than what you know consciously. As God is all knowing, and never gives you less than what you ask for. For God (superconscious mind) searches your conscious mind and makes better arrangements for you, as it is referred to in Romans 8:26-28. When awareness is born, the right actions are automatically produced as the body produces the right chemicals, including dopamine, and all the strength that is needed to drive the manifestation of the new awareness. Awareness produces automated action with little to no effort.

Finally, when I give you my awareness as an answer to a specific prayer, know that you only get the awareness or Principle that directly relates to your prayer. For example, if you ask me for a shirt, I can show you where to find one to buy, and I can show you where to get other things similar to or related to a shirt. Or I can show you how to make a shirt, etc. But I will not show you or give you the awareness of how to make a rocket ship, unless you passionately pray for that as well.

To further enhance your understanding, let's go ahead and talk about the different levels of awareness.

Me: Okay.

God: There are seven levels of awareness, namely:

1. Passive or General Awareness

2. Lukewarm Awareness

3. Self-Centered Awareness

4. Active or Inquisitive Awareness

5. Faith-Based Awareness

6. Intuitive Awareness

7. Pure Awareness

1. Passive or General Awareness

This is the basic level of awareness. Everybody has this type of awareness. People at this level of awareness are aware of things that appear in the physical and are aware of basic causes and their effects. However, people at this level feel that they have no power to change the causes of their life to manifest the effects they desire. The prayers of people at this level are generally centered around ordinary thoughts and wishes.

As a result of their prayers not reaching a passionate stage, they live as victims of life, and they feel that everything just happens to them without their consent. Even though all people experience the effects of their own causes, people at this level feel that they are not responsible for the effects that they experience. They feel that something external to them is causing all their effects. And they don't realize that their own actions are the causes that create the effects that they experience. Consequently, people at this level usually believe that lucky breaks in life may come to them, but there is nothing that they can do to change when they happen. As a result, they feel helpless and don't know what to do to make positive changes in their lives.

2. Lukewarm Awareness

This type of awareness is almost the same as passive awareness. The difference is that people at this level of awareness know that they have the power to change the effects of their lives. But they do not really care to study to understand and organize the causes they know of, so that they can be coordinated and replicated to produce their desired effects. People at this level just don't have the inner drive or motivation to change the effects of their lives. At this level, even though you may not understand all causes, you will sometimes unintentionally cause things to produce an effect that you desire. However, because your prior effect was unintentional, you will likely lack the will to systematically organize the causes of your prior effect to reproduce more of the effects that you desire. This is because you sometimes understand certain Principles or causes subconsciously. So your subconscious mind takes control to get you to do things that bring you certain effects even though your conscious mind is not aware of the associated Principles or the Word.

3. Self-Centered Awareness

This type of awareness is similar to lukewarm awareness. The difference is that people who have this awareness *do* care to understand and organize causes or Principles so that they can replicate them for their desired effects.

However, their prayer manifestation is often delayed because they have the feeling that they know it all. As a result, they regard other people's opinions on Principles as not useful. It is common to have a delay in manifestation for people at this level, even when their prayers are at either the stage of a desire, or a passion, due to their constant indifference to wisdom from others. People on this level generally make all their decisions based on their self-interest and do not consider how much their decisions will affect others or how others will perceive them. Sometimes they may appear to be arrogant due to their strong resistance to learn or accept relevant knowledge from sources outside themselves. People that have this awareness are able to make some headway in life, but they are not able to achieve much due to their constant tendency to rely solely on their own knowledge versus other cutting-edge knowledge that can point them to untapped awareness within themselves.

4. Active or Inquisitive Awareness

This is the same as self-centered awareness except that people that have this awareness are very humble. And they possess a strong will or desire to listen to other people's opinions. As a result, they obtain other people's knowledge and carefully observe many real-life examples of causes and effects, in order to systematize these causes to create the effects they desire. People who are at this stage of awareness are very curious about causes. And causes, as you know, are the same as my Principles, the Word, or God or myself. At this level of awareness, people **use higher levels of imagination to combine and/ or permute different Principles that they know about to create the effects they desire.** Generally, many of the prayers of people who are at this level of awareness are at the stage of either a desire or a passion.

Anyone who has an active awareness eventually seeks to find more Principles to lead him or her to God, the ultimate Principle (superconscious mind). This is the basic level of awareness you need to attain in order to begin noticing the answers to your prayers. Even though I answer all your prayers, if you do not have active awareness, you may not know that your prayers have been answered. This is because people without active awareness do not pay attention to the causes or Principles that I use to manifest things around them. So they think all good unintended effects are just "lucky breaks." At this level of awareness, you will experience many positive aspects of the law of attraction simply by you paying attention or by you seeking. You do not have to be religious to experience this type of awareness. Many successful people have this type of awareness, and they believe that they are the cause of their success. As a result, they take time to analyze and harness many causes or Principles (Word or God), and they put the right causes into action to create the effects they desire. However, active awareness has limitations, as it can be very frustrating if you do not have an immediate understanding of certain causes or Principles. It can also be very time consuming, and perhaps expensive, to gain the knowledge of the causes or Principles needed. When you find yourself limited by this type of awareness, then you will need a faith-based awareness to gain further knowledge of the causes that you desire to know about.

5. Faith-Based Awareness

Faith-based awareness is not a belief in any religion. It is an *active* awareness, as I just described above, and a simple belief in the power of either the Universe or God (one's subconscious and Superconscious). A person with this awareness believes that he or she is connected to God or the Universe and thereby connected to infinite knowledge that can be called upon for assistance. As a result, people who are at this level are characterized by extreme hope, even in the face of adversity or temporal setbacks. They fall seven times, and they rise seven times. They don't give up, because they know the universe will bring them what they pray for. And they know that all things are working together for their good. At this level, you will easily recognize your subconscious orchestrating the delivery of both physical and nonphysical items to you. These items may be knowledge, or causes, or Principles from the people around you, or Principles from your environment, and even Principles from your experiences. Also, you will easily recognize synchronicity and serendipity, which are by no means coincidences. People who have this type of awareness usually have their important prayers at the stage of passion.

At this level, you will feel very powerful due to your connection to Infinite Intelligence, which is the source of everything. Yet, you will also feel very humble, as you will know that your power is based on the power of the universe, which is love. It is worth mentioning that many people on your planet have this awareness, and yet, they have no religious affiliation. Again, you do not have to be religious to possess faith-based awareness. Awareness in itself has nothing to do with religion. You can be extremely religious and only possess general or passive awareness, and you can be nonreligious and still possess faith-based awareness. Even though faith-based awareness is good, what you really need in order to start experiencing an extraordinary level of fulfillment is *intuitive awareness*.

6. Intuitive Awareness

Intuitive awareness is produced by the regular or consistent use of faith-based awareness along with the following daily practices: The first is meditation, relaxation, and physical exercise. And the second is your study of causes, through books and close observation of people and the things that matter to you. As you practice intuitive awareness on a daily basis, you will begin to notice a pattern with your awareness. This pattern will help you to put two and two together on many issues very quickly. In other words, you will start figuring out other causes with little to no effort at all.

Also, at some point in the development of intuitive awareness, your dreams will merge into your waking consciousness, and you can see yourself in more than one place at the same time. This is sometimes called lucid dreaming. You will begin to see the future and make corresponding changes before it happens. At a very high development of this awareness, you will begin to see and hear what only prophets and psychics see and hear. On a regular basis, you will start to figure out different manifestations of awareness without having had any direct prior experience of that awareness. This is because you will be getting help from higher spiritual forces that are part of me. It is very common at this stage to move so fast with using your intuition that it will appear that you are on the super-fast lane of awareness.

Me: Whoa! So how fast can I move on the fast lane at this level? Can I go like 200 miles per hour, or a thousand miles per hour? Is there a limit? And if I pass the limit, will there be a policeman to give me a ticket?

God: You can go as fast as you want on the fast lane.

Me: Wow, that sounds really exciting! Can I go so fast to the point of even overtaking Jesus?

God: Hmmm, you know, as far as overtaking Jesus, you might get a ticket for doing so; so you may want to watch your speedometer.

Me: Oh no, why not, I was not going to overtake him by so much that he could not see my back; just five or ten miles.

God: I thought you were only going to pass him by a mile, but if you try five miles, you may get multiple tickets.

Me: Oh no! That's not fair!

God: Seriously though, you can go as fast as you want without getting any ticket. I was only kidding with you. Even Jesus wants you to go as fast as you want to. Jesus knew you could do so, and that is why he said, "He that believeth in me, the works that I do shall he do also; and greater works than these shall he do because I go unto my Father" (John 14:12).

Me: That's a relief to know.

7. Pure Awareness

God: Pure awareness is the realization of all causes and their effects. It is the realization of all the awareness we have talked about and more. It is the source of all awareness. It is the awareness of all the Principles, or the Word of God. And since you know that the Word of God is God himself, it should be clear that pure awareness is the awareness of God. To be fully aware of something is to understand the cause of it and how to replicate it anytime you choose. This level of awareness is the highest form of awareness. It is the beginning and end of all things. It is pure potential and the source of infinite possibilities. When you pray, I answer your prayers by giving you bits and pieces of this awareness. Over a period of time, or a lifetime, or lifetimes, of practicing intuitive awareness along with deliberate expressions of pure love to as many people as possible, you will be able to gain the full awareness of God. When you have this awareness, you will know for certain that all things are possible.

I desire that you gain this awareness. We will always be one, whether you know me or not. However, when you fully obtain this awareness, you will know without any doubt who you are, who I am, and who we are, and that we are all one. This was, and is, the desire of Jesus for you. Could you read for me what is written in your Bible in John 17:20-23?

Me: Sure. It says: "I pray also for those who will believe in me through their message, that all of them may be one, Father, just as you are in me and I am in you. May they also be in us so that the world may believe that you have sent me. I have given them the glory that you gave me, that they may be one as we are one - I in them and you in me — so that they may be brought to complete unity. Then the world will know that you sent me and have loved them even as you have loved me."

God: So what Jesus was praying for was that you would gain pure awareness of yourself and all that is in and around you. Pure awareness is simply my Word in totality. It is again my Principles or my truth. It is who I am, and who I have been, and who I will always be. When you gain this full awareness, you will know that you are in me, and I am in you, and that we are one and inseparable. Buddha also recognized this truth and knew that all things are one and that is why he is also quoted as saying: *"...I have seen deeply that nothing can be by itself alone, that everything has to inter-be with everything else. I have seen that all beings are endowed with the nature of awakening."* So again, you can see that we are inseparable, even if you don't know it. But you have the power to know the truth when you desire to know, or to be awakened.

It is impossible to have this awareness by accident. The only way to have this awareness is to desire it and to work towards it passionately. To have this type of awareness is to know the cause of all things. When you are passionate about having this awareness, you are essentially praying for it. And since passion is effective fervent prayer, your passion will definitely, and eventually, avail much.

Me: This sounds so beautiful. I definitely desire to have this awareness. However, it sounds very far-fetched, as I do not know anyone who has been able to achieve this. How do I start?

God: Quite a number of people have achieved this awareness, and you can too. Simply start by praying for it passionately. Practice intuitive awareness as I described, and love all people. Also, tune in during the day to hear my voice and study my Word. Study my Word carefully, and divide it carefully with all your heart and mind, so that you can know my truth for you. And so that you will know which truth to apply at what time to get the best results. I will be speaking to you through your heart, but also through your experiences, the hearts of your friends, the hearts of your family, and all that you come in contact with, so be on the lookout. Pay attention. Pay attention. Pay attention. Pay attention. Listen to the still small voice within you for clues to causes, and know that this type of awareness resides right in you at all times. It is within your reach because it is within your own superconscious mind. And it's just a matter of you tapping into it. Of all the things you can do to attain pure awareness, just desiring it passionately will propel you to people, places, and things that will help you to attain it faster.

Me: Is this type of awareness the same as cosmic consciousness or unity consciousness that Maharishi Mahesh Yogi talked about?

God: Many people have called this type of awareness with many names. There are so many forms of awareness within pure awareness. Many have described the awareness that they know of, but I tell you that there are more Principles or forms of awareness within pure awareness that is far beyond your current comprehension. For now, however, know that both unity and cosmic consciousness can be found within pure awareness.

As you gain more and more of pure awareness, I will be coauthoring many more books with you.

Me: You mean this is not the only book I am going to write? I have not even agreed to write another book, and you have already made the decision without me? I thought you gave me free will, and now it appears you are trying to pull some kind of gangster move to force me to write another book without you asking me!

God: Take it easy now. You don't have to write another book or even finish this book if you don't want to.

However, whether you like it or not, as you gain more and more of this awareness, people will flock to you to gain a little of your awareness, and in that sense, even without you writing a book, your life will be a book in itself. If you don't write a book, others may look at your life and write a book for you. So, rest assured that I was not trying to pull a gangster move on you.

Me: Okay, that makes me feel relieved. So you are essentially saying that as I gain more and more of pure awareness, I will become a book-making machine?

God: Yes.

Me: This is some great stuff I am getting from you. I really believe that this has the potential to make people more joyful and make them millions of dollars if they follow the instructions for gaining awareness that you have shown me in this book. People can use this to pray to get what they need much more easily. Would it be okay if I charge $10,000 for each copy of this book?

God: Whoa! Now, this is some real gangster move that you will be pulling on people if you charged $10,000 per copy. How much did I charge you?

Me: Aaaaaaah, aaaaaaah, aaaaaaah, nothing.

God: Exactly my point.

Me: Okay, okay, fine. Not to change the subject on you, but you just mentioned that I should study as well to help me to get pure awareness. Can you tell me what to study?

God: First of all, you cannot change the subject on God, as God remembers everything and can, therefore, come back with the subject anytime. But anyway, to answer your question, study everything around you. However, use the majority of your time to study the things that relate to your desires. For example, if you want to be a doctor, then in addition to praying about this desire, consider doing the following: Find a school that teaches about how to become a doctor; observe and study your own body to see what gets you sick and how you heal; search for a doctor that you can talk to, so you can get some insights into the field; etc. Make sure to get enough answers such that you can formulate your own truth. Also, study spiritual books. A good source to start from is the Bible, but don't end there. Observe, observe, and observe. Ask, ask, and ask. Seek, seek, and seek. You cannot observe, ask, or seek enough. As you observe, ask questions, and seek answers to your desires, you will find my Principles at work all around you, through people, things, and places. Everything you come in contact with, or experience, are my Principles at work, so you cannot miss my Principles. Observe the effects around you, and sooner than later you will discover many causes. By finding and using the causes around you, you will be increasing your awareness; but most importantly, you will *become* the awareness, or the causes that you discover. In other words, you will be the cause, and once you are the cause, then you can choose when to be the effect at your own timing. To say that you will be the cause and the effect is the same as saying that you will be the beginning and the end, or the alpha and the omega of the cause, or the awareness that you have.

In conclusion to pure awareness, it should be clear to you by now that the thoughts you generate or have, eventually become what you believe in. And what you believe in, eventually becomes what you can see with your mind. And what you can see with your mind, eventually becomes what you know, or are aware of. And what you know eventually creates your reality, which is your state of being, or awareness. **Once you are done with any state of being or awareness, you can move on to a different state of being, and the way to do that is to pray, and use faith to transport your prayers to God.** Let me restate this in a different way. The vehicle you use for movement from one state of being or awareness to another begins with an ordinary thought, then to a wish, then to a desire, and then to a passion. You accelerate this movement by faith. Once you reach the state that you desire and obtain the awareness of that state, you can then create the desired state as many times as needed. All this begins with a single thought which comes from your imagination. So you are only limited by your imagination.

Me: So you are saying that I can change my state of being over and over, as many times as I desire, and my imagination is the limit?

God: Yes.

Me: Okay then, I will do this over and over, and the skies will be my limit going forward.

God: Well, there are no limits. Rather than the skies being your limit, let the universe be your limit.

Me: Wait a minute. I'm confused. You just said there are no limits, and now you are saying that the universe is the limit. So there is, in fact, a limit to what I can imagine. Right?

God: To say that the universe is your limit is the same as saying that you have no limits, because the universe is ever expanding and therefore has the size of infinity.

Me: Wow, that is amazing!

God: So keep on having higher and better thoughts about

who you want to be. Keep on imagining your desired state, over, and over, and over, and soon you will find yourself there. Repeat it again, and again, and again, for this is what life is all about. This is what produces the thrill and the joy of life. This is creation. This is my Word. This is my Principle, and this is me in action. This is God.

Me: You are really, really, wonderful!

God: Thank you, and so are you. Now, let's look at the vehicle that you need in order to quickly move your ordinary thoughts to a passionate stage and a higher level of awareness. This vehicle is called *faith*.

CHAPTER 4

FAITH

Faith is made up of three components, which are vision, believing, and action.

Your *vision* is simply what you desire, or what you are passionate about. You know what your desires are, so they need no explanation. Let me therefore explain what *believing* is, and what an *action* is, relative to your faith.

The first thing I would like to point out is that the word "believing" is a verb and not a noun. Consequently, "believing" is a word that *does* something. Believing is the act of exercising a belief. Whatever you are believing in is your belief, and that particular belief is a part of your whole belief system. To believe is simply to *expect* something. Expecting something is *doing* something. Everything that happens in your mind is a spiritual action, so your act of believing or expecting is an act of doing something in the spiritual realm. In the spirit realm, what you believe in happens instantaneously. In other words, you get your desire, or your belief fulfilled immediately. That is to say your prayer is fulfilled immediately in the spirit realm.

Consequently, you must always maintain the confidence, or the assurance, that *what you are believing in is done* even before you see the corresponding physical manifestation.

Abraham Lincoln recognized the importance of believing. This is why he said: "To believe in the things you can see and touch is no belief at all, but to believe in the unseen is a triumph and a blessing." This is also stated in the Gospel of Mark 9, verse 23, as "All things are possible for one who believes." You can transfer your fulfilled prayer in the spirit realm to the physical world through the continuous imagining of your fulfilled prayer with gratitude and ACTION. Once you understand that what you are believing in is already fulfilled in the spiritual realm, all you have to do is to take action to bring it into physical manifestation.

Other than believing, there are two types of actions that you can take to manifest your spiritually fulfilled prayers. The two actions are direct and indirect action.

Direct actions are immediate physical actions that you take towards the achievement of your desire. For example, if you want to be a doctor, then you will take the direct action of going to school to learn how to be a doctor. If you don't have the money to go to school, then you will look for a scholarship by asking the people you know, or have access to, for information about scholarships or assistance programs.

Indirect actions are physical actions that are not directly related to the physical manifestation of your prayer. However, you take these actions to demonstrate that you have already obtained what you believe in. For example, if you have a belief of having obtained abundance in the spirit realm, then you can demonstrate this belief by dressing like a rich person, relaxing like a rich person, and behaving in as many other ways as possible that models abundance rather than lack.

In order for your faith to work, the three components above must be *very active*. In other words, your belief in what has happened in the spiritual realm must be ongoing and firm, and you must continuously take direct and indirect actions to transfer your spiritually fulfilled prayers to the physical realm.

Me: You stated that in the spirit realm, what you believe in happens instantaneously. If this is the case, then why do I have to keep on believing to transfer what I believe into the physical realm?

God: It is like drawing a picture that you see on a wall on a piece of paper. To draw it, you first look at the whole picture on the wall. Then you look at a small part of the picture and hold it in your mind. Once you have a small part of the picture captured in your mind, you then draw it. And then you switch your attention back to the whole picture on the wall to capture another small part of the picture to draw it. You repeat this process until what you are drawing looks exactly like the complete picture that you see on the wall.

The act of continuously believing works the same way. In the analogy I just described, the act of looking at the whole picture and capturing a small piece in your mind for drawing is the act of believing. And the act of drawing on paper what you have captured in your mind is faith in action or a direct action. If you don't repeat the process above, your picture will not be fully drawn. Repetition of the process is the only way to guarantee the drawing of a full picture.

In the same way, you must practice the act of believing in your prayers by repeatedly looking at the picture of your spiritually fulfilled prayers in your mind. And then take direct and indirect actions incrementally to bring your spiritually fulfilled prayers into physical manifestation. There will always be some negative circumstances or challenges around you. Yet, in the midst of all challenges, if you don't continuously practice the act of believing or seeing in your mind that your prayers are already fulfilled, then you cannot bring your spiritually fulfilled prayers into physical manifestation. If you believe one moment and then stop believing another moment, then you will lose the picture of your fulfilled desire, which is necessary for you to draw it out or translate it into the physical realm. If you say that you believe in something, but cannot see it fulfilled, then it is impossible for you to translate it into the physical realm, as you will not be able to see it to draw it out or manifest it. You must therefore not lose the picture of your spiritually fulfilled prayers, as that will make it hard for your prayer to be manifested. The only way to not lose the picture of your spiritually fulfilled prayers is to continue to believe, and to continue to imagine what it would feel like to have your prayers fulfilled.

Me: That is a great analogy. But it sounds like I have to do all the work by myself by first having a vision, believing in the vision, and taking actions to bring my vision into manifestation. I thought that is what God is for. What role does God play in my life then, as I am doing all the work by myself?

God: My son, you are not doing all the work by yourself. The work that you do by having faith is less than one percent of the reason that you are able to manifest your prayers. Yet, your less than one percent effort is very significant, as it is your less than one percent effort that draws my attention to arrange the opportunities and circumstances for your prayers to be manifested. Think about the wisdom I give you daily, the air that I give you to breathe, the strength that I give you, the intuition that I give you, the people that I send to you daily, and many more things I do that we cannot exhaust in this book. I am definitely your true partner, who never lets you do the work by yourself.

Me: Thank you for the reminder. I think I lost track of all that. You are so right. You are truly the best partner I have ever had. Thank you for all that you do for me.

God: You are welcome.

Me: Back to the subject of faith. I certainly have a vision or an idea of what I desire in life. I certainly have imagined my desire as fulfilled in my mind before, and I have been taking actions toward the manifestation of my desires each day. But every now and then, my faith reduces, and I feel helpless. And I feel that what I imagine as fulfilled is just some mere fantasy and not real. I sometimes feel that you may not be paying attention to all the times that my faith was strong or when I believed in you the most. Sometimes it's hard, and I feel like when I over-believe, I might let myself down, as you might not answer my prayers.

God: I certainly understand how you feel. However, let's look at your concern from a different angle. Remember that faith is like a *vehicle* that carries your prayers to God and then returns your answers. The vehicle of faith must keep on moving at a faster speed so that your request can reach God quickly and return with his response quickly.

Most luxury and expensive vehicles require premium fuel for better performance over the long run, and so does your faith. Your vehicle of faith requires many premium fuel combinations or accelerants to produce the best speed and to guarantee better performance in the long run.

There are many premium fuels or accelerants that you can use for your vehicle of faith, but for this book, I would like to discuss 17 that I believe will be of great help to you. The **17 accelerants** are so powerful that when you put them in your vehicle of faith, they will accelerate your speed and increase your faith beyond your imagination. Any time that you feel down or think that you are low on faith, come back to this book. Then reread all the accelerants to increase your faith, as reading them is like taking medicine to increase your faith. The moment you reread and practice them, your faith will soar back up. And then you will be able to manifest your prayers or desired outcomes faster.

By using any of the following accelerants, or a combination, you will essentially be exercising your faith, and the answers to your prayers will be moving much faster toward you. Let me list the accelerants, and then we will go through each accelerant to discuss how you can use each one to increase your faith:

Faith Accelerants

1. Appreciation or Gratitude
2. Feeling
3. Do something
4. Relax
5. Meditation
6. Listen to or read the Word of God
7. Listen to, sing or hum encouraging music
8. Giving
9. Think the opposite of undesired physical realities
10. Act the opposite of undesired physical realities
11. Daily affirmations
12. Expectation of desires
13. Expectations and time management
14. Continuous improvement through observation
15. Right environment
16. Encourage others to gain faith
17. Grace

Now that we have them listed, let's go through them one after the other.

1. Appreciation or Gratitude

God: When you appreciate something, you add value to it or cause the thing that you appreciate to increase. Both "Appreciation" and "Gratitude" mean to add value to something. If you do some research, you will find out that the word *appreciate* means to raise the value of something. And to have *gratitude* means to increase the value of something you are pleased with. Therefore, when you show appreciation or gratitude, you are not just being thankful, but rather, you are spiritually and physically increasing the value of what you are appreciating or pleased with.

Jesus knew this Principle very well, and that is why he showed appreciation before performing many of his miracles that are recorded in your Bible. For example, he thanked God for five loaves and two fishes before feeding the multitudes, because he knew that he could not feed five thousand people with the five loaves and two fishes he had in hand without first appreciating them to cause an increase (Matthew 14:19). He knew that appreciation was a faith accelerant that can push one's prayer quickly to God to bring a quicker manifestation. When you lose appreciation of what you currently have in the physical and the spiritual realms, you block yourself from receiving what you are praying for.

Me: But sometimes, it's really hard to express appreciation for the things that I have because I am so used to having them that it's very easy to take them for granted.

God: I know. It is when you take things for granted that you start to lose more of the things that you are not appreciating. One way to generate appreciation for what you have is to consider for a brief moment this statement: How do others, who are hopelessly trying to possess what you already have feel like? They are probably not too happy that they don't have what you have. When you realize that you physically have what others desperately desire, quickly switch your attention to what it feels like to have what you currently have by remembering the benefits that you have derived from what you have, and by anticipating any other benefit that you can derive from what you have. Then, you will realize how blessed you are to have what you have, and then feel a sense of appreciation. Be careful when you do this type of comparison to ensure that you do it for the purpose of appreciating yourself and what you have, and not for depreciating or looking down on yourself, as others may have more than you have physically. So, for the purpose of appreciating what you have, compare yourself with those that you feel may have less than what you have in the physical realm. And for getting inspiration or a sample picture to imagine your fulfilled prayer, you can also compare yourself with those who have more than what you have. You do not have to imagine *being* other people; instead, you can imagine what it will feel like to understand the Principles that help them to produce the effects that they have. The moment you gain appreciation, your faith will naturally soar up; and you will become more receptive to receiving answers to your prayers.

In general, there are three main types of gratitude or appreciation relative to personal belonging or things. The first type is the act of physically expressing gratitude for the things that you possess physically. The second type is the act of mentally expressing gratitude for the things that you possess physically. And the third type is the act of mentally expressing gratitude for the things that you possess in the spiritual realm that are not physically manifested yet.

Let us first discuss what it means to physically show appreciation for what you physically have in your possession. To do this, you have to intentionally add value to what you have by taking simple improvement actions such as cleaning, re-arrangement, adding accessories, replacing worn-out parts, painting, changing the functional use of one thing for another, spending time to read about other uses of what you have, etc. Sometimes, you can discover big inventions by your conscious attempts to physically engage, and add value to what you have. This is why it is said that necessity or deprivation is the mother of invention.

Second, to mentally appreciate something that you have, you will need to look at it and recount all the times that it has been useful to you. You will also have to look at it and creatively imagine and count all the potential useful benefits you can derive from what you have and express gratitude in your mind. This is what is meant by the popular saying: "Count all your blessings day by day." But I tell you what, count your blessings hour by hour and then minute by minute. And when you do this, you will not only see your faith elevated, but you will also notice a faster manifestation of your prayers. As you express sincere gratitude for the things that you have, you will be causing an increase in the spiritual realm and an eventual increase in the physical realm.

The third type of appreciation is the act of mentally expressing gratitude for the things that you possess in the spiritual realm that are not physically manifested yet. To be grateful for the things that you have in the spirit realm, you must first imagine that your prayers have been fulfilled. It may appear that your prayers have not been fulfilled or answered, but the Bible says that even before you ask, God will have already answered (Isaiah 65:24). Therefore, since I have already answered, what is needed is for you to enjoy the imagined feelings of having your prayers fulfilled while you express gratitude for what I have done. You can take your mental expression of appreciation of the things in the spirit realm to the next level by physically acting out how you feel. For example, if you mentally appreciate a car in the spirit realm, you can act it out by taking a driving exam or by buying a leather polish for your car's seat.

Here is a big secret. In showing appreciation for the things I have provided or done, take note of every small thing I do for you and express gratitude for it. Failing to see the small things is failing to see the big things, because the big things are made up of the small things. If you show appreciation while looking at the small things, and simultaneously show appreciation for the big things that you see with your imagination, you will set the law of attraction in motion to bring you more of the small things that you see.

You cannot effectively express gratitude for a provision that you cannot imagine. That is why you have to see the small things and imagine what it will be like to have more of the small things. In doing this, try to imagine your prayers as already fulfilled and thank God for it. What does it *feel* like to see in your mind your fulfilled prayers? It's a beautiful feeling, isn't it? If it's not quite clear how beautiful the feelings are, then let's take some time to discuss what it means to *feel* your fulfilled prayers. Incidentally, that is the next accelerant on our list.

2. Feeling

God: Feelings are originated from your conscious and subconscious mind level. On your conscious mind level, you generate feelings by using your five senses and your imagination. On your subconscious mind level, feelings are generated through past programming or belief systems, meditation, and your sixth sense. Let's discuss feelings that are generated on your conscious mind level, and then we will discuss feelings that are generated on your subconscious mind level.

On your conscious mind level, in order for you to perceive or feel something, you first have to use one of your senses. You can do this by seeing, smelling, hearing, touching, or tasting. Regardless of which of the five (5) senses that you use, the feeling is produced in your conscious mind. To have faith is to believe. And believing includes your ability to *feel* that your prayers are already answered. In order to feel that your prayers have been answered, you have to use your conscious mind to imagine what it will be like for your five senses to perceive or experience your fulfilled prayers. The clearer you can imagine your prayers as fulfilled, the more natural and easier it will be for you to experience what it would feel like to have your prayers fulfilled, even though they have not yet manifested. For example, if you want to generate the feeling of having a new home, you can imagine seeing the new home with your eyes; walking through the rooms of the new house with your legs, turning on the lights in the rooms and observing them with your eyes; walking in the backyard and smelling the flowers that have been planted; walking in the bedroom, or any room, and hearing your favorite music playing; sitting down on the sofa and feeling the comfort of the sofa; cooking in the kitchen; opening the refrigerator to get something to eat; etc., etc.

When you imagine, try to use all your senses and do in your imagination the same things that you desire to do when your prayers are manifested. Also, imagine what it would feel like when your loved ones see you having, and using your spiritually fulfilled prayers. When you imagine with your five senses as described above, you will automatically generate a feeling that matches, or is at least similar to the feeling you will have when your prayers are physically manifested. As you imagine having, using, and feeling your expected answers to your prayers, express sincere inner gratitude for the feeling. Are you listening?

Me: Oh yes. I am.

God: Okay, pay rapt attention to what I am about to say, as it contains a very important secret.

Me: Okay.

God: The act of imagining is the act of thinking, and thinking always produces thoughts. Feeling happens only because you think or have a thought, and each thought is a prayer. **If each thought is a prayer, then it presupposes that a feeling is a prayer, since a feeling is produced as a result of a thought.** So you can see that feelings are the climax of any thought, and the climax of any feeling is passion. The Bible says that "The effective fervent prayer of the righteous availed much" (James 5:16).

Let us break down the above scripture, so you can get the secret from it. The word **fervent, as used in the above** scripture, means intense or persistent or persistent pas-sion. Since the word "fervent" means "persistent," let us try to replace the word "fervent" in the above Bible quo-tation with the word "persistent." And then, let's replace the word "prayer," also in the above quotation, with the word "feeling." By doing so, the above Bible quote will read as "**The effective persistent feeling of a righteous person availeth much.**" **Look at the re-written quotation again and again, and you will discover a hidden secret.** The secret is, *your feelings are your prayers, but your feelings must be persistent to produce results.*

This is what Saint Paul also expressed by saying that you should pray without ceasing (1 Thessalonian 5:17). When you produce a feeling for something, you only have to repeat the feeling a few times daily to make it persistent. Repeating the feeling simply means that you should replay the thought that led to the initial feeling in your mind. Once the thought is repeated a few times dai-ly, you are guaranteed to have the same feeling again. And over time, that feeling will become a passion. Remember that from a physical standpoint, God answers *passionate prayers* before he answers all other forms or stages of prayer that we have discussed. If feelings are the climax of any thought and passion is the climax of all feelings, then passion or persistent feelings are the highest form of prayer you can ever offer.

So it is important to try to have as much of the feeling of your fulfilled prayers daily. Doing so will be an act of fervently praying, which will definitely avail much. To ensure that your prayers are fervent, make sure that you mentally switch your attention from the undesirable things that you see or experience each day, to your spiritually fulfilled prayers. Each moment you think about something that you do not like (which is a prayer), immediately switch your mind to think about what you desire (which is also a prayer). The more you do this, the more the prayers about your desires will become fervent. The mastery of your feelings over time will bring you so much success that some people will think you have been using some voodoo powers. Do you understand all this?

Me: I do. Thank you.

God: Now let's look at how you can change your feelings on your subconscious mind level. I stated earlier that you can change your feelings on this level by using past programming (belief systems), meditation, and your sixth sense. Let's first talk about belief systems and your sixth sense. We can talk about meditation later, as it is one of the faith *accelerants* that we will be discussing.

Each day, bits of data enter your senses, and they are then passed through your belief system for interpretation without your conscious awareness of the process of interpretation. Your interpretations of the bits of data form your thoughts or perceptions, and your thoughts in turn, create your feelings. If you want to change your feelings, you have to change your belief system, as your belief system is the *filter* for all your thoughts. Your belief system comprises of all your experiences, what you have ever read or heard that you like, dislike or disregard. It is simply all your prior thoughts that have been put into three categories: The first category are the things you agree with, or your ideals; the second category are the things you do not agree with, or your non-ideals; and the third category are the things you neither agree with, or disagree with.

Put differently, a belief system is a collection of beliefs and/or assumptions. Your belief system can make you feel either good or bad for any new information or bits of data that you get. For example, you may have a belief that money is the root of all evil. Because of this belief, any time you hear about someone desiring to be a millionaire, you may think that the person has a bad desire, as his or her desire will ultimately lead to evil. However, what if you change your belief system by accepting that money is not the root of all evil, and then accept that what you do with your money is what could lead to evil? Then you will no longer demonize money as evil. And you will be able to easily welcome the desire or thought of becoming a millionaire as good.

You can start changing your belief system by simply evaluating new information. This is what the Bible refers to as: "study to show yourself approved, a workmanship that is not afraid but rightly dividing the Word of truth"

(2 Timothy 2:15), so that you can seek the perfect will of God. To be able to rightly divide the Word of truth, you will have to make an effort to introduce new information to yourself *before you need the new information.* You do this by reading and observing events around you. You also do this by observing accomplished people that you admire, and the Principles or causes that they practice. You can also do this by carefully observing your own experiences to form reliable opinions of the experiences. Finally, you can do this by *listening* to accomplished people that you admire. Once you have any new information, ponder over it. And then decide what you believe in and what you don't believe in. The outcome of your pondering will form an addition or a replacement to one or more of your existing beliefs.

A good belief system contains the type of beliefs that can help you to positively filter your thoughts to give you the right perception that you need. The right perception will help you to achieve your goals and to be in harmony with the universe. Therefore, to change how you feel on your subconscious level, intentionally update or add to your belief systems daily. Add newer and better beliefs regularly, so that you can unconsciously use them to positively filter your thoughts as needed.

As I stated before, your belief system is the same as your *past programming.* Another way to change your beliefs on the subconscious level is to use affirmations to ensure that any *new* belief that you come up with is internalized or accepted by your subconscious. Once your subconscious has accepted a new belief, it will automatically go to work to produce the feeling associated with your new belief, as needed.

Finally, you can use your sixth sense to produce the feeling of your fulfilled prayer. This takes some practice. Your sixth sense is your connection to your superconscious mind, the source of all things. You maintain your connection to your sixth sense by maintaining a conscious connection to your subconscious mind. Based on your prayers, your superconscious sometimes delivers nuggets of wisdom or Principles to your conscious mind through your subconscious mind. These nuggets of wisdom or Principles will come to you in the form of hunches, impulses or nudges. Once you hear these nuggets of wisdom or hunches, your body will automatically produce a feeling. This type of feeling produces the peace that transcends all understanding. In Philippians 4:7, it is said that this type of peace guards your hearts and mind. You cannot explain this feeling because its root is from your superconscious mind.

As you practice hearing from me on a daily basis, you will get more of this feeling. This is one way your superconscious mind talks back to you. When you begin to feel good about something, without having consciously made an effort to have that particular feeling, pay attention to your feeling, because you will find some Principles associated with it. These Principles will generally contain inspirations and instructions on what to do to manifest what you are praying for. The inspirations or instructions you receive are what is sometimes called "intuition."

When your intuition speaks to you, you will need to do something about it. So let's look at what it means to do something that you have been inspired to do by your superconscious mind through your subconscious mind.

3. Do something

God: Do something related to your prayers or vision each day. It does not matter whether what you do is big or small. Just do something. For example, if your prayer or desire is to run a thousand miles, then just start by running a half mile or even a quarter mile. The moment you start running, I will give you more strength to run a little further, and then a little bit further until you get to your destination. It is virtually impossible for you not to get an impulse to do something when you have the feeling I just described. If you are still confused, then simply go to your nearby university or vocational school, or to an accomplished person that you admire, and ask for guidance. You will notice that the moment you do one little thing, that one little thing will lead you to do another little thing, and then another. This will continue until you achieve what you are praying for, or what you are passionately desiring.

Even though it's important to do something, it is equally important to ensure that you have enough time for *relaxation*, which is the next faith accelerant for us to look at.

4. Relax

God: This may sound very contradictory to the above, as the above says you have to do something. However, to relax simply means: Do not try to over-think or do much more than necessary. This also means that you should have fun doing the things that you do for a living. And you should also set aside some time to enjoy your favorite recreational activities such as playing table tennis, pool, or golf, or doing fun things with your family, etc. This is very important because the very act of taking your attention off your work puts your subconscious in control of your work.

Your subconscious mind has more knowledge about your work than your conscious mind does, so let it do some of your work for you while you play. If you fail to relax, your subconscious will have very limited opportunity to help you in getting your work completed. It is extremely important for you to develop trust in your subconscious. To trust in your subconscious means to make time to relax and have fun. To trust in your subconscious is to trust in God, and to trust in God is to have faith in God. Many of your modern-day breakthroughs came about with the help of the subconscious. Failing to set time to relax or enjoy yourself will be setting yourself up for mediocrity. To trust in your subconscious, is to trust in God because your subconscious is part of God. The act of relaxing is a message to God that you know he is in control, and as a result, you do not have to worry or do too much. When you do too much to the point of stress, or act like you can consciously take care of all things, that means that you are telling God to back off.

Remember that it is not how much, or how fast you work, or what you do. But rather, it is how much you depend on God to direct you on what to do. And also know that much more direction from God will only come to you when you relax. This is why the Bible says the race is not for the swift nor the battle for the strong nor does food come to the wise or wealth to the brilliant or favor to the learned; but time and chance happen to them all (Ecclesiastes 9:11). Time and chance are only fully controlled by God or my Word. So learn to lean on the Lord or my Word for direction, and don't overwork yourself.

Me: Oh wow! This is very fascinating! I guess this explains the famous phrase: "Eureka! Eureka!" (I found it! I found it!) that Archimedes shouted when he discovered the Archimedes Principle while relaxing in a bathtub.

God: Yes, and notice that Archimedes only got his answer when he was not busily working. Also, in addition to relaxing, take time to meditate. The importance of meditation cannot be over-emphasized, so let's discuss that next.

5. Meditation

God: Meditation is a powerful faith accelerant. To meditate is to spend some time in silence without doing anything, while focusing your attention on one thing, ideally your breath. A simple meditation that you can do is to simply sit quietly, close your eyes, and just try to listen to the sound of nature or your breath. Many people meditate by sitting quietly on a chair in their homes, or by sitting outside in nature. Meditation will help improve your whole body and improve your awareness or consciousness of spiritual and physical truths. Meditation will improve your ability to hear my voice. After consistently practicing meditation for some time, you will become more joyful and happier, and you will tend to be calmer, even in potentially stressful situations. Meditation will also improve your intuition. Just like relaxation that we spoke about earlier, the act of meditation is an act of *faith*, as it is an act of surrender to God. When you surrender to God, you put God to work for you. The benefits of meditation are many, and more than we can discuss in this book, so do further research and experiment with different types of meditation to find out what works best for you.

Meditation is so important that scriptures have been written to underscore its effect, but only a few pay attention to it. For example, Exodus 14:14 states that "The Lord will fight for you; you need only to be still." And Psalms 46:10 states that "Be still and know that I am God." So as you can see, one way to get me to work for you is for you to do nothing for a moment or for some time. You only have to be still and believe in me.

Me: So how long should I meditate?

God: You can start with a daily meditation practice of 5 minutes. Then, when you feel ready, you can do a 10-minute meditation for some time, and then 15 minutes for some time, and then however long your subconscious directs you to do. However, I suggest you do not meditate so much that you have no time to deliberately engage in prayer or no time to *do something* towards your passion. Regardless of what you do, ensure that you keep a routine, and don't jump from a 5-minute meditation to an hour meditation habitually. Also, be consistent for a while before you change your meditation time. If you are going to meditate for 5 minutes, try to stick with it for a little while, and be consistent to build a habit.

6. Listen to or read the Word of God

God: You have been told in the Bible that faith cometh by hearing, and hearing by the Word of God (Romans 10:17). This is very true. As you go through your day, what do you listen to or read? These days, there is a proliferation of my Word. You do not have an excuse on where to find it, as technology has made it more readily available. My Word is all around you and within you. It is on the internet, radio, television, etc., etc. You are made up of the Word. The Word is your DNA. Remember that, in the beginning was the Word, and the Word was with God, and the Word was God, and without the Word was nothing that is made that was made (as expressed in John 1:1).

It is out of the Word that you came from. The Word is my Principles, and so *you* are my Principles. You just need reminders and a personal passion to find out who you are, and once you do, you will know that you are my Word. When you find out that you are my Word, you will become a full embodiment of it in your daily life through demonstration. Then, you will be able to say what Jesus said, which is that you are the way, the truth, and the light, and no one can come to the Father except through you.

My Word is all that there is, so study it. And as you study it, you will be able to use it to manifest all your prayers or create anything that you desire. As you listen to or study my Word, you will gain faith and strength to overcome any negativity or difficulty in life. My Word is light, and it is capable of illuminating any darkness or difficulty in your life. My Word is the solution to any problem or difficulty you can ever imagine. When you study my Word and use it, you can claim that ...you are more than a conqueror...(Romans 8:37).

Me: I'm confused about what the difference is between the Word and God. How can God be just a Word or Words?

God: Good question. The Word of God describes who God is and how he operates. If you understand how God operates based on his Word, you will be able to harness the power of God. Even though the Word describes who God is, the Word itself is not independent of God because the Word is a pointer that points to God. Imagine having a ball that contains something valuable inside it. And also imagine that the ball has something written on it that describes what is inside the ball and how to get it. The writing outside the ball is part of the ball, yet it describes what is inside the ball, of which it is part of as well. When you get the instructions outside the ball, you can then go within the ball to get all that is within. That is why I have sent you teachers to remind you of what is inside you, as you sometimes may not see what is written on your body, which is the ball. All the Word is within you because you are made of it, but you do not remember your makeup, and that is why you get frustrated in life. Take time to study the Word in order to understand what is within you, and you will discover that you are capable of manifesting anything that you desire or pray for.

Therefore, remember my Word in all things. And remember that all the accelerants I am giving you are parts of my Word. Since it is out of my Word that you were created, you are also my Word. This means that these accelerants are already part of you, and you can activate or experience them whenever you are ready. The accelerants are very powerful, and they can be taken as medicine either separately or combined. They are more potent when combined than when they are separated.

Me: Wouldn't it be an overdose if I take all the accelerants at the same time?

God: Not at all. The more you use these accelerants, the happier you will become, as you will experience more prayer manifestations in your life. And the more you use these accelerants, the more your faith will grow.

Me: You know, sometimes, when I feel down, I say to myself: "If only I had enough time, I would be able to listen to or study the Word of God all week long to accelerate the answering of my prayers." But it's really hard to find time to do so.

God: Well, based on where you desire to be right now in your life, doing so may cause an overdose for you, and you may need to be treated in the hospital for it. What you need to do is to set some time aside each day, like an hour, or two, or three, or more, to study. Then use the rest of the day to go about your daily activities. Also, know that you can study my Word even while going through your daily activities by closely observing the workings (or Principles) of things around you, as all things are made of my Word. My Word is everywhere, so observe it wherever you are.

My Word will inspire you, correct you, rebuke you, and train you to be righteous. That is to say that my Word will make your outside body shine like your inside body, or my Word will cause you to operate with integrity. To operate with integrity is to do the things that all of your three minds (conscious, subconscious, and Superconscious) desire the most at any given moment.

When you get the Word, you will be more than an overcomer. My Word will bring you power, my Word will bring you joy, my Word will bring you security, and my Word will make you courageous. When you have the power that comes from the Word, you can walk through the valley of the shadow of death and fear no evil. The

Word is knowledge, and the Word produces wisdom, so get it, and you will have what is said in 2 Peter 1:2, which is that "Grace and peace will be yours in abundance through the knowledge of God and Christ."

Finally, let me give you a big secret that has eluded men for many generations. Are you ready?

Me: Yes.

God: Okay. Did you know that studying or reading my Word is the same as praying to me?

Me: How is that possible?

God: Let me ask you a question. When you study or read anything, do you use your mind to process or think about what you are reading or studying?

Me: Yes, I do. Oh, wait! Wait a minute! I think I got it. Are you saying that the act of reading or studying produces ordinary thoughts, which form the basis of all prayers?

God: Bingo! You are spot on. Your studying or reading produces ordinary thoughts, and you already know that ordinary thoughts form the first stage of all prayers. If you happen to read a book that goes a little deeper into a single subject, then by the time you are done reading it, you would have had many repeated ordinary thoughts about a single subject. These repeated thoughts can form a wish, then a desire, then a passion, and then a higher level of awareness. When you feed the desire or passion that you develop as a result of reading or studying a given subject, you will eventually have a higher level of awareness. And when you do, you would say to your self: "Wa-laa!" (Voila!). As you will be seeing your prayers getting manifested even before you can think about the "*hows*." This is so because every ordinary thought that you get through reading or studying is amplified by me through the law of attraction.

Therefore, when you run out of what to say, or what to do, or when your faith is down, simply let your intuition guide you to find my Word about your desires in a book. Then study the book, and divide the messages or implied lessons you find in the book into three categories: What you believe in, what you do not believe in, and what you do not have any opinion on but will seek to understand later. And before you know it, the knowledge that you obtained from the book will be amplified by me, and your faith will soar up. Studying, reading, or listening are not just prayers in themselves, but also, they are the *seeds* that create passionate prayers - "...that availeth much" - as stated in the Bible. Jesus taught his disciples the importance of ordinary thoughts. When you have time, look up the parable of the sower, and you will realize that Jesus called ordinary thoughts as mere "seeds" or "the Word."

Me: My Goodness! This is so simple, but also very profound!

God: Yes. It is. It is so simple that many people think that it is foolishness, or they just don't take it seriously enough. But the wise man delights in gaining understanding of my simplicity on a daily basis.

7. Listen to, sing or hum encouraging music

God: Listening to encouraging music is like listening to my Word, except that the flow of the music makes your body move. Or, it at least creates in you a desire to want to move your body. Do this anytime, whether you feel down or up; but especially when you are down, or feel that your faith is low, and this will help increase your faith.

If you do not have a device to play encouraging music, sing your own encouraging song to yourself, or hum an encouraging song whenever possible. Especially when you are confronted by something negative, either physically or in your mind. This is very effective; try it whenever you are down, and you will notice that your faith will definitely rise up.

8. Giving

God: Giving is a core signature of God. Everything that God does is about giving, and so should you, as you are made in the image of God. Giving is a powerful faith accelerant. When it is applied correctly, it can get your prayers answered very quickly. However, due to a misunderstanding that surrounds giving, the rewards for giving remains very elusive to many people. To understand how giving works, and its importance, you have to understand how giving relates to appreciation and gratitude – which we discussed earlier. Do you remember me telling you that when you appreciate or show gratitude for something, the thing being appreciated increases in value?

Me: Yes.

God: The same thing happens when you give, but even more. You give only because you care. What you care about is normally what you appreciate. The reason you give to someone is that you care about the person's welfare. The act of caring means you appreciate the person. Any person who appreciates what you give to them, immediately causes you to have an increase in the spiritual realm and an eventual increase in the physical realm as well. If you understand this, you can reverse-engineer appreciation by genuinely giving to many people that need your help to earn their appreciation. When you earn someone's appreciation, you earn an increase for whatever you gave. The increase that you get from someone appreciating what you give is usually way more than what you originally gave. This is what the Bible means by "Give and it shall be given back to you. A good measure, pressed down, shaken together and running over..." (Luke 6:38).

Me: So what happens when I give to someone who does not appreciate what I give?

God: If you give to someone who does not appreciate what you have given, you will earn back little to none of what you gave. This is why Jesus said that: "Do not give dogs what is sacred; do not throw your pearls to pigs. If you do, they may trample them under their feet, and turn and tear you to pieces" (Matthew 7:6). This also means that you should not waste good things on those who would not make a profit on what you give. Profit here means appreciation. When someone appreciates something, the person gives a spiritual and a physical value to what he appreciates. By giving a value to what is given, a value is automatically attached to the source, where the thing came from. The person you give to does not necessarily have to do something for you in return in order for you to receive back what you gave. Although this can happen as a bonus, your real reward, which is pressed down and shaken together, will come to you from multiple angles that are orchestrated by God.

Me: Okay, so what exactly can I give to earn appreciation?

God: You can give anything. But remember that it is important that you really, truly give from your heart. Give because you want to give and not because you feel an obligation to give. Give because you care. Caring is truly loving. The person who genuinely cares, and gives to another as a result, is a true demonstrator of who God is. This person is directly rewarded by God. It is not possible to be God and have nothing. So it is said that: "For God so loved the world that He gave his only begotten son that whoever believes in Him should not perish, but have everlasting life" (John 3:16). I understood, and I still understand giving. I knew, and I still know, that the only way to get more people to come to me is to give myself, so I can have many sons and daughters, including you. You can also give yourself to others by giving your time, attention, care, love, money, smiles, knowledge, wisdom, products, services, etcetera, etcetera. Most importantly, give out superior business services or products in exchange for money or whatever is mutually equitable.

Me: Wow! But tell me, other than business products or services, how much do I have to give?

God: Only give what is from your heart. Give to yourself first, but make sure to reserve a portion of what you earn to give to others. A portion can be 5 percent, or 10 percent, or 15 percent, or even all of what you make. The key is to give what is from your heart, and to give to those who will appreciate what you give. Once you attain a higher level of spiritual understanding, you will not worry anymore about how much you are to give, as you will know that you can never run out of what you have by giving. A higher spiritual understanding guarantees that the more you give, the more that you should receive. Giving gives birth to appreciation or gratitude by others, and appreciation or gratitude by others gives birth to an increase for you. The very act of someone appreciating something in his or her mind, for what you have given without any words, is a seed for the opening of spiritual blessings for you.

Me: That's a beautiful answer. But the Bible says we must give a minimum of 10 percent of our earnings as a tithe. So, isn't what you are saying somewhat contrary to what the Bible says, since you are also alluding that I can give less than 10 percent?

God: No. What I am saying is not contrary to the Bible. What I am suggesting is that you should strive as much as possible to give 10 percent, and even more as you gain spiritual understanding. But if you don't have 10 percent or more to give, then make sure to give whatever is from your heart. This could be 5 percent or a lesser percentage of your earnings. And remember that God loves a cheerful giver. Also, remember that the more you give, the more you can receive. But give based on what you have and what you are cheerful about giving. And you will be rewarded according to what you give and the level of cheerfulness or inner joy attached to it.

Now let me point out a secret to you. When you are cheerful about something, it means you are happy about something, and it also means that you appreciate whatever you are happy or joyful about. Do you remember what I said about appreciation again? Your cheerfulness is a form of appreciation because your cheerfulness causes an increase or appreciation in the person you are giving to. It is this appreciation, along with the appreciation of the person who receives, that magnifies what you give, to come back to you in a form that is "...pressed down, shaken together, and running over" (Luke 6:38).

Me: Wow! Thank you for the clarification.

God: You are welcome. And because you appreciate what I just told you, I can assure you that you have activated an increase in the quantity of my spiritual Principles that are coming to your conscious understanding.

9. Think the opposite of undesired physical realities

God: It is certainly okay to admit what you see physically that may not be desirable. When you admit the undesired things that you physically see in your mind, your vibration gets lowered or changes to match what you see. This means that *what you see is who you are*. It's the same thing as saying that the observer is the same as the observed. Since you do not want to be the undesired things that you see, it is important to only admit what you see for a brief moment in your mind, and then switch your attention to see what your fulfilled prayer or passion would look like in your imagination. By so doing, you will change your vibration from a lower frequency to a higher frequency; and consequently, your fulfilled desires will move towards you quickly. For example, whenever you see or think about your bank account being low in funds, also make sure you think about the abundance of money flowing into the account to fill it up. Whenever you think about your business not having enough customers, also think about more customers being directed by God to come to your business. By so doing, you will neutralize the initial admission of the physical reality and cause the spiritual reality that you see to move towards you quickly. Failure to think the "opposite" of your undesired physical manifestations will cause that which you are seeing or thinking of to repeat itself, *as all creation starts from what your thought is focused on*. When you think the opposite of undesired physical realities, you shift your low faith level to a high or increased faith level.

10. Act the opposite of undesired physical realities

God: In the same way that it is important to think the opposite of undesired physical realities, it is also important to act the opposite of undesired physical realities. For example, if your bank account is low on funds, but you need to pay for marketing for your business, you can act the opposite of this physical reality. By faith, you can take actions such as asking the marketing company to offer their services at a discounted rate, or to offer their services and be paid at a later date, or even to exchange services between your business and theirs if possible. You could also ask a friend for a loan to pay for the services. By so doing, you are making decisions that are not based on lack, or a negative or zero bank account, which was caused in the **past** and is persisting in the **present**. But rather, you are making decisions that are partially based on the **future**, which is faith that the money is in the bank account, or at least, the money is flowing to the bank account. Where is the **future**? It only exists in your imagination. The only way to experience the future is to act the opposite of undesired physical realities. That means that you do not wait for the future to happen to you, but rather, you cause the future to happen on your timetable.

By acting in this way, you are creating physical resources based on things you do not see. Put differently, by acting the "opposite" of undesired physical realities, you are creating out of the thin air. When you act the opposite of undesired physical realities, you open yourself up to experience serendipity and synchronicity of miracles. It is impossible to live a life on the physical plane that has not already been lived in the spiritual plane or in your imagination. So to live a better life in the physical realm, you must first endeavor to live the desired life in the spiritual realm – through your imagination. Imagine, and imagine, and imagine possibilities; and sooner than later, your imagination will become your reality. You are limited only by your imagination. Using your imagination and acting on your imagination is the same as living or operating in the spiritual realm. So be creative.

11. Daily affirmations

God: To affirm something means to state something as true or a fact. Technically, it is not necessary to affirm something to yourself if you already know that it is true. However, the reason that you have to affirm ideas or concepts to yourself is that *you have forgotten who you are*. That is to say that you do not remember your direct connection to God. Therefore, when you affirm something that is not physically manifested, you are only trying to bring into your conscious awareness what God already knows about you.

I have placed everything that you would ever pray for within you, but you are not fully aware of this yet. Consequently, it is challenging for you to affirm that you are strong when you know that you are weak. However, if you believe that everything is possible with God, and you believe that everything you need is inside you, then all you have to do is to repeat what you want to be to yourself over, and over; and sooner than later, both your conscious and subconscious minds will believe what you are saying or affirming. What do you want to be? A doctor? An artist? A politician? A singer? It does not matter. Just keep repeating to yourself as often as possible that you are the person that you want to be, and you will soon find out that you were right all along.

Me: But what if I wait till I become what I want to be before I tell myself what I am? Wouldn't that be more honest?

God: Yes, that would be honest, but it will not be less honest if you say it before you become it. As I stated, everything that you want to be, you already are; but you are just not consciously aware of it. When you repeat to yourself that you are something before you see it manifested, you are admitting to a universal truth. Even though it may be hard to believe at first, by repeating that you are your affirmations, your conscious mind will eventually accept as true and believe what you are repeating to yourself. Once your conscious mind believes what you are saying, your subconscious mind will in turn believe what your conscious mind believes. Then, your subconscious mind will go to work to bring into existence what you believe in. At that point, all you have to do is to pay attention to the promptings you get from your subconscious mind. In some instances, you will not even have to pay attention. What you believe will just happen through the law of attraction without you doing anything.

Your politicians know this very well. Have you ever seen a politician lie on TV over and over? And then, before you know it, people, including yourself, start believing the politician?

Me: Yes, yes, yes! I get it.

God: Good. That is the same thing that cheerleaders do for their teams. Use affirmations even when you doubt, and before you know it, you will start believing in your affirmations. When any one of your affirmations becomes a belief, that belief will activate your faith. And your faith will activate your subconscious mind to produce the desired solution to manifest your belief. Once your subconscious mind is activated, you will be unstoppable in the pursuit of your affirmations that led to your beliefs. You can say your affirmations either verbally or non-verbally (in your mind). However, it's good to do both because they each have different frequencies, and therefore, they have different effects. So it is said again in your scriptures that "Let the weak say I am strong" (Joel 3:10). You do not have to be strong before you call yourself strong. You can look at it as a lie, but again, if you lie to yourself enough times, your lie will eventually become your truth. So continuously affirm your spiritually fulfilled prayers to yourself, and sooner than later, they will become physically fulfilled prayers, and your faith will increase.

12. Expectation of desires

God: To expect is to look forward to something happening. When you pray, you should expect that I will answer your prayers. If you do not expect that I will answer your prayers, then praying is not quite useful for you. However, if you believe that I will answer your prayers, then you should expect or look forward to answers from me. In exercising expectation, one key thing to remember is that the desired outcome can come in so many forms and from so many directions. So do not limit what you expect and where it will come from. Make sure to be on the lookout for answers from everywhere and anybody you meet. Some people will clearly not have answers for you, but they may *trigger* the answers that you desire. When you expect positive things to come your way, you *activate* the positive aspects of the law of attraction in your life.

Me: I like to always expect positive things to happen, but it is sometimes difficult. Many times, I kept expecting, and expecting, and expecting positive outcomes, but when things did not go the way I wanted, it got really frustrating.

God: The reason why things don't go the way you want is that you first get frustrated that it is taking too long. Secondly, even though you should go about your day expecting good things to happen for you, be open to *all possibilities*. And be assured that no matter what happens, I will be with you to ensure that you are more than a conqueror. My ways are not your ways, and I know better how to direct your affairs. Getting frustrated when you don't get what you expect means that you have become too attached to what you are expecting. When you become too attached to what you are expecting or to your desired outcome, you put God in a box, and you thereby prevent him from doing the exceedingly abundantly above what you can think and imagine. Getting frustrated means that you have taken things into your own control without fully considering my Principles. Getting frustrated means your faith level has gone down.

Keep your faith up all the time for I will never let you down. Don't be too attached to your expected outcomes, but rather, be attached to me. Being attached to me means that you should be interested in learning more about me and how to practice or use my Principles. When you focus on learning about me and practicing my Principles without any attachment to how and when the outcome you desire will come through, you will open yourself up to receive answers from unexpected sources that will cause your faith to soar up. Over time, as you practice what I am telling you, you will become more interested in my Word, and that in itself will bring you more joy than the outcomes you desire. This is what is meant by the popular Biblical saying: "...seek first the kingdom of God and all things shall be added unto you" (Matthew 6:33). The kingdom of God is the Principles of God that we have been talking about. As you maintain your expectation of God acting or showing his power from all directions, it is also important that you manage your time carefully. When you manage your time carefully, you will be able to control your expectations. And thereby, you will be able to control any potential frustrations from even starting. Therefore, let's look at expectation and how it relates to time management.

13. Expectations and time management

God: Have two sets of expectations *each* day. The first set of expectations should include what you want God to do. These should be expectations that are exceedingly abundantly above what you can think or plan to achieve. The second set of expectations should include your plans for what you think you can *reasonably* accomplish. It should include your general routine tasks and at least, one or two faith-stretching tasks.

Faith-stretching tasks are tasks that are related to your short, medium, or long-term desires or prayers. As the name suggests, they are tasks that help to stretch and increase faith gradually. There are two main types of faith-stretching tasks. The first type includes tasks that are *within your reach* that you have not done before. And the second type includes routine tasks that when carried out, they have a build-up effect that will eventually thrust you into the fulfillment of either your short, medium or long-term prayers. Faith-stretching routine tasks are different from general routine tasks in the sense that your general routine tasks are usually urgent, and they must be carried out in order to keep your job or whatever assignment you have. Whereas faith-stretching routine tasks are usually not urgent but are related to your short, medium, or long-term prayers. It is important to ask yourself this question every morning: "Does my task list or to-do list for today include a faith-stretching task?"

Also, it is important that you create expectations that you sincerely believe that you can reasonably achieve. Otherwise, even if God does something unreasonably exceptional, you will most likely not know that God has done something. This is because you cannot know what

God does that is unreasonably exceptional, if you don't first know what is reasonable.

Once you have two sets of expectations: one that is based on what God can do, and another that is based on what you can reasonably do, then go out and do what you can reasonably do. But while you are doing what you can reasonably do, believe that God will intervene to help you exceed what you can reasonably expect or imagine. To work on your reasonable expectations, while you wait on the expectations that are based on what God can do for you, is the very act needed for you to take control of time and reduce frustrations.

Your reasonable expectations must be prioritized and written down. And they must be crossed out upon completion and reviewed each night, or evening. Over time, as you practice carefully reviewing the variance in your daily expectations and your achievements, you will notice that God does something for you each day above what you expect. Even if what God does for you each day appears to be little, by noticing it each day and expressing appreciation for it, your faith will naturally grow. Once you start noticing the little things that God does for you each day with appreciation, before you know it, the little things will turn into something exceedingly abundantly above what you can expect or imagine. Setting your expectations is the same as time management. To manage time, simply write down all that you desire to accomplish, and write down a detailed list of what you can reasonably do to achieve them on a daily basis. It is important to ensure that you have a prioritized list with the approximate time that it will take to accomplish each task. For example, if you say that you will go to the grocery store to buy some supplies, and it is a priority, then you have to ensure that you make it a priority, and define how long it will take to accomplish this task. Over time, you will become an expert on assigning the exact or approximate time that you need for any task that you have. Once you have all your tasks listed with time allotments, you will know the total time that you need to accomplish all your tasks. If the total time needed to accomplish all your tasks is more than your total working hours for the day, then you need to reprioritize your tasks. And then shift some of your tasks to the next day. Or you could also look for help, or find more efficient ways to get all tasks done on the same day. Also, make sure to reserve a little bit of time for miscellaneous tasks that may come up during the day.

Me: So you are essentially saying that if I plan my day with time allotments, I will invariably be able to achieve at least my reasonable expectations unless something more important comes up.

God: Yes, and if something does come up, just reprioritize your day, and you will feel that you are in control. It is important to ensure that you do not overbook or overschedule yourself for the day as that will bring you frustration. Do one thing at a time. You will reduce frustrations and feel that you are in control when you use my Principles. And when you reduce frustrations, your level of faith will rise up. God does not need you to overbook or overwork yourself in order for him to abundantly exceed what you can think and imagine. When you overbook yourself for the day beyond your reasonable expectations of what you can do, that means that you do not have faith or trust that God can do more with less. Therefore, do just enough during the day, and ensure that you do not overbook or overwork yourself, as that will cause your faith level to go down. Finally, also set a short-term or medium-term expectation for say three months, or six months, or a year, and make sure that your reasonable daily expectations are directly tied to it. And as you go about your day, make sure that you are using the best technology or know-how available. To do this, we have to talk about continuous daily or weekly improvement.

Me: Can I say something before we talk about continuous daily improvement?

God: Yes.

Me: This is great information. I believe anyone that finds and uses this information will have much more control of their day. This reminds me of a book I once read with the title of "The One Thing," by Jay Papasan and Gary Keller. What you are saying here appears to be similar to what I read in that book. Is that a book that you would recommend?

God: Yes, that is a great book, but like any other book, do not take what the book says as your final truth. Instead, make sure to think about the concepts and try them out, and then come to your own truths, as that is the best way to learn.

Me: Okay. Thank you.

God: So let's move on to continuous daily or weekly improvement, as it is directly related to your time management or your setting of expectations.

14. Continuous improvement through observation

God: Ask yourself as often as possible this question: "Is there a better way to do what I am currently doing?" The answer may not always be obvious to you. But still ask the question over and over, because your question is a prayer in itself. When the repetition of your question or prayer increases to the level of passion, your question will be on God's priority list. And once your question or prayer is on God's priority list, it is a done deal. The answer will come in the form of awareness. When you get an awareness or a Principle or a new idea about any particular question, execute your new awareness by putting the Principle into practice, and then monitor the result. Upon execution, ask yourself again if there is a better way to do things based on your new awareness, and repeat the above process until you get what you desire. The above process is what has become popularly known as a "feedback loop."

Repeat your feedback loop through a never-ending process of implementing your awareness and then observing your awareness in action. Then review your results, ask questions, and start your feedback loop again by using your new awareness gained from your prior questions. Do this over, and over, and over, and you will be guaranteed to become the best in whatever you do.

The better "**ways**" to do the things you are doing are parts of my Principles, or my ways, or myself. Even though I always answer your prayers, you do not always recognize the answers because of your low awareness or lack of knowledge. The more awareness you acquire, the easier it will be for you to hear my voice, know my promptings, and recognize my Principles in action. When you gain awareness, it will be easier for you to spot my Principles in the area of effective tools or best practices for your work. If you need help on gaining the needed awareness for spotting my Principles, then consider enrolling in seminars, vocational schools, or courses that have something to do with your line of work on a regular basis. And you will notice that one idea will lead you to another. This is why I told you that all my Principles cannot be contained in the Bible. Many of my Principles are taught in all churches, universities, mosques, technical schools, and all institutions of higher and lower learning.

Me: Did you mention mosques as well?

God: Yes.

Me: Well, while growing up, I learned that I had to tolerate people from different Christian denominations and people from different religious backgrounds. But I was also informed that my religion or denomination was better than everyone else's denomination or religion. Why then would you say that the mosque will have something good to teach me? Are you asking me to be open-minded and even learn from people with different denominations or religions?

God: Yes. Any Principle that you learn that is an expression of love to you and all people is my Principle. Don't limit yourself to learning from only one place; learn from different places, and compare and contrast the lessons. Through your comparing and contrasting, you will find what is good and acceptable for you. This is what is meant by: "...be transformed by the renewing of your mind. Then you will be able to test and approve what God's will is – his good, pleasing and perfect will" (Romans 12:2). You cannot know what God's perfect will is if you do not know what is *not* God's perfect will. You cannot test something if you do not know what can be considered failure and what can be considered success. You have to have two opposing ideas in order to test what is pleasing for you. This implies that you have to consistently compare your work tools and practices to other tools and practices, and see if there is something new that you can learn to improve yourself or your work. Do not be ashamed if the new practices or ways are not popularly accepted. Simply be open-minded, look at other practices, and take the practices that you think will be helpful to you, and leave the ones that will not be helpful to you. In fact, the Bible even encourages you not to be ashamed to learn from other practices for the purpose of contrasting and finding what works for you. This is exactly what is stated in 2 Timothy 2:15: "Study to shew thyself approved unto God, a workman that needed not to be ashamed, rightly dividing the Word of truth." The Word of truth, as I stated to you previously, is not limited to the Bible.

Me: But there are people out there spreading false messages. So how do I know the truth?

God: I know what you mean. But, the phrase "false message" is somewhat misunderstood. There is no message out there that is false, except that some messages work for certain circumstances and the same messages do not work for other circumstances. My truths work the same way. If you apply my truth wrongly, it will not work, and if you apply it the right way, it will work. But it is all my truth. All that exists are my truths, or my Word, or my Principles. The false messages out there are simply my truths applied in a way that is different from your perspective. It is also my truth applied in a way that may not satisfy your personal desires, aspirations, or prayers. Sometimes, you can gain a wealth of wisdom just by carefully allowing yourself to observe people who may appear to be misapplying my truths. This type of wisdom may be forfeited if you superficially or blindly say that someone else's religion is false or bad without doing a careful examination yourself. A word of caution must be exercised when saying that a given truth is misapplied because my truth can be applied in so many ways to get the same, similar, or different results. *You cannot go wrong if you look for **love** in all things, and do unto others as you expect them to do unto you.* Whenever you are introduced to any new truth, simply ask yourself if that truth expresses *love;* and if it does not, you will know that it is simply my truth applied in a way that is not particularly beneficial for you. Therefore, consistently look for better ways to do your work, even if it means you have to go to the mosque to learn something. By the way, here is something you can learn in mosques: Do you know that many committed Muslims go to their mosques to pray five times a day?

Me: Yes.

God: Why do you think they do that?

Me: Well, now that I have the understanding of what a passionate prayer is, I suppose that one of their reasons is to increase the level of their prayers to a passionate state for a speedy answer.

God: You got it. This is one of many things you can learn from mosques. This is why I told you to be open-minded and look for the practices that are beneficial for you. The more you improve your tools or practices, the more confidence you will gain in the process of asking, seeking, or praying. And the more confidence you gain in the process, the more you will have a positive forward-looking perspective. A positive forward-looking perspective will definitely cause your faith to soar and bring you what you desire faster. Sometimes, you do not even have to go anywhere, as the answers will be right in front of you, but if you do not ask or seek, you will not find it. Follow your intuition, and you will be fine. Your intuition will lead you to the perfect or right places or environments that have the answers you desire. With that said, let's talk a little bit about the right environments.

15. Right environment

God: The whole earth is one big environment. Within this big environment, there are sub-environments known as countries, cities, towns, suburbs, etc. Within each sub-environment, there are further sub-environments like stores, playgrounds, homes, places for entertainment, etc. All sub-environments have been purposely created to serve mankind and to produce different results. All sub-environments are good, but not all sub-environments are beneficial to you, relative to your prayers. If your prayer is about wanting to be a pilot, then what use is it for you to be in a place that will not give you an opportunity to practice what you want to be? How do you expect me to show you how to fly an airplane if you don't go to an environment where you can find an airplane to practice with?

Me: But you are God, and you can easily cause an airplane to drop from the skies to me.

God: Yes, I can, but that will go against my Principles. Besides, if I dropped an airplane from the skies to you, don't you think that it would be unfair to everybody else? My love for you is the same as my love for everyone else. If I give you everything you pray for without involving your conscious physical contribution, then there will be nothing for you to do.

It is important that you locate yourself in the right environment, relative to your prayers. This is why I plant mango seeds only in places that will support the growth of mango trees. To accelerate the answering of your prayers, go to places where you can see samples or examples of what you are praying for. The samples will increase the intensity of your desire or prayer. The samples will help elevate your prayers to a level of passion. The more you see, hear, touch, smell, or taste samples of your fulfilled prayers, the more you will be activating the feeling of having your fulfilled prayers.

The more you have the feeling of having your prayers fulfilled, the more your five senses will be receptive to listening for instruction from your subconscious on how to manifest your prayers. The more you can sense samples, the more you will appreciate the samples; and the more you appreciate the samples, the more you will be increasing the rate at which the samples manifest themselves in your life. What samples of your fulfilled prayers are you sensing each day? Do you intentionally go to places that have samples of your fulfilled prayers for sensing or feeling? Do you have pictures of your spiritually fulfilled prayers on your walls at home or at work to help you reactivate the feelings of your fulfilled prayers? Are you hanging around people that drive your attention away from your spiritually fulfilled prayers? Your answers to these and similar questions will determine how fast your prayers will be answered.

Finally, whenever you pray, go into the most conducive environment or place to express your prayers.

Me: But what is the most conducive place to pray?

God: The most conducive place to pray is the place where nobody can physically see you, and it is where there is order and organization. Jesus referred to this place or this environment as your closet or your room in Matthew 6:5.

Me: But how can I go into my closet or room to pray continuously and still be able to go out and *do something* towards the manifestation of my prayers? If I pray in my closet or room only, how would I be able to pray without ceasing as advocated by Saint Paul and many other sages?

God: Jesus was not literally referring to your closet or room as the place to pray. But rather, he was referring to your mind. Your mind is your closet or room. Your mind is the place where nobody can physically see you. When you learn to pray in your mind, you will be able to pray without ceasing. You can pray in your mind at work, at home, while dancing, while eating, while playing, and at all times. Your mind is your secret closet. This is the closet where all masters pray fervently from; and not necessarily a church, or even an altar. Consciously enter this closet every moment. And you will be in the presence of your father, who can see everywhere, and hear everything, even in the secret places. *When you enter your secret closet, start your prayer with a thought, then raise your thought to a wish, then to a desire, and then to a passion. Then rest assured that I will hear your voice in your mind.*

Me: Thank you.

God: Finally, as much as possible, ensure that your closet is well organized before you pray, as that will speed up the repetition of your prayers to the level of passion.

Me: How do I do that?

God: One way to see how organized the closet of your mind is, *is* to look at your home and your office. Are your home and office well organized and clean? Your home and work will be well organized to the degree that you are well organized in your mind. A disorganized home or workplace is a sign of a disorganized mind.

Therefore, to organize your mind, start by making a conscious and progressive effort, to organize your home and office. A well-organized mind is a mind that does not have clutter. When your mind is well organized, you will have fewer distractions. And fewer distractions will make it easier for you to quickly move your prayers to the stage of passion – through repetition. Also, fewer distractions will make it easier for you to hear my voice to get directions on what to do to manifest your prayers, and thereby increase your faith. Additionally, a well-organized home, office, and environment, especially ones that have samples of your spiritually fulfilled prayers, offer many benefits. For example, it will help you to think clearly, stimulate the intensity of your prayers, and consequently increase your faith by causing a faster manifestation of your prayers.

Furthermore, you can organize your mind by meditating or being still. And you can also organize your mind by writing down your plans, goals, or vision, and by creating a to-do list on a daily basis.

Me: What an explanation! Thank you for the clarity.

God: You are welcome. So, to recap how to achieve the ideal prayer environment to increase your faith, practice the following: Go to places that have samples of your fulfilled prayers. Associate with people who will encourage you relative to your prayers. Clean and organize your home as well as your office to free your mind from cluttered thoughts. And write down your vision and to-do list to clear the environment of your mind.

Once you have the ideal prayer environment, and you have meditated to clear your mind, then enter the closet of your mind to pray without ceasing. And gradually, your faith will soar up like never before.

16. Encourage others to gain faith

God: Encouraging others to gain faith is one of the most powerful accelerants for increasing your faith. It works instantly. Take notice of those who may be going through seemingly difficult situations that you can offer to help either through your kindness or your words of encouragement. Provided the person you intend to encourage is receptive, you will notice your own faith soar during and after the period of your encouragement. This is due to a spiritual law that states that you can never run out of what you give. The more you give, the more you will receive. Try this out, and you will be amazed.

17. Grace

God: I reserved the most powerful faith accelerant for last. *Grace* is my unmerited favor. My grace is an unmerited favor because I do not give it to you based on what you do. Rather, I give it to you based on your *genuine attempts* to know me. My grace contains the power that you need to accomplish anything. Everybody has access to my grace, but the measure of grace that you receive is directly proportional to your *genuine attempts* to know me. It is one thing to have access to my grace, and yet a completely different thing to use the access that you have. Even though all people have access to my grace, many people only use a basic level of my grace. A deeper level of my grace will only come to you when you attempt to know me.

To know me is to know my Word, and to know my Word is to know my Principles. When you know my Word, you will gain a deeper awareness of me. And a deeper awareness of me will give you a deeper level of my grace. And when you have a deeper level of my grace, you will have a deeper understanding of my love for you. And when you understand my love for you, you will gain power to accomplish anything you can imagine.

I cannot stress enough the importance of my Word. My Word is all that there is, all that has been, and all that will forever be. It is what you are made of, and it is what everything is made of. When you gain more understanding of my Word – either through the Bible, prayer, observation, dreams, life lessons, or through any school – and then *apply* my Word, your measure of grace will increase. My grace is there to compensate for your weakness. Do not intentionally try to be weak, and expect my grace to be abundant for you. This is because I can see your heart, and you will be rewarded according to what is in your heart. Also, bear in mind that grace is not necessarily made available because you know all my Principles. Rather, it is made available by your *persistent, genuine attempts* to be better through the learning and the using of my Principles. This is why Paul said, "... Grace and peace will be yours in abundance through the knowledge of God and Christ" (2 Peter 1:2). A higher knowledge of God and Christ will only come to you if you attempt to know God and Christ. **Your persistent, genuine attempts are the keys to access my grace. To know my Principles on an intellectual level is good, but it is much better to know my Principles by applying them in your own life, or by observing other people apply them in their lives.**

Therefore, even though it is very important to study all the accelerants we have discussed, make sure to apply them in your life daily. But if you forget something, know that my grace will be available to you. If you forget any of the accelerants, simply come back and reread it, and try to apply it again. Your attempt to remember and apply my Word will be greatly rewarded with more grace, beyond what you can dream of. My grace is part of my faithfulness. In all your ways, fear not, worry not, and know that I will never leave you nor forsake you. For I am one with you in all your experiences. We are a team. It is my grace that turns all physical additions into multiplications. When you come to me with, say a faith level of two, I will give you, say a grace level of one thousand, to augment your faith. And if you come to me with, say a faith level of three, I will give you a grace level of three thousand, to augment your faith. You do not necessarily earn my grace since you already have my grace. But you get to use more of my grace by simply trying with a pure heart to know me. I am a rewarder of all those who diligently seek me. To diligently seek me, means to be passionate about seeking me. And to be passionate, as you know, means to be praying fervently. And to pray fervently means to be on my priority list. Therefore, pray to me by faith, and know that before you even ask, I will have already answered through my everlasting grace. **And whenever you feel weak or discouraged, remember that "My Grace is sufficient for your weakness" (2 Corinthians 12: 9). This remembrance is so important that at the mere recollection of it, your faith will soar.**

Me: Thank you so much for reassuring me with your Word. Well, I guess I should say *our Word* since I am made of it too.

God: You are absolutely correct.

Me: That is so comforting. Thank you.

Follow-Up Questions on Faith

Me: I believe the above accelerants are very powerful, and I have been trying to apply them since you brought them to my attention. But every now and then, I still find myself thinking about the negative and the things that I do not desire. For example, I am believing in you to create a breakthrough for a situation that my family is facing, and somehow my mind keeps drifting to consider all the possible negative outcomes. I know I have faith in you, and I don't want my mind to drift to my undesired outcomes, but it does. I feel like the more my mind drifts to the undesired outcomes, the more my faith reduces. This really messes with my psyche, and it makes me feel that all the faith I have is nothing. And this further makes me feel that I am just lying to myself.

God: I can help you to appreciate what is happening better, but first, let me ask you a question. In addition to praying, have you physically done everything you can possibly do that you know how to do?

Me: Yes.

God: Okay. If you have done all that you can physically do, then the rest of what you can do is spiritual, and this happens right in your mind. Remember what I said about faith. I told you that your faith is *the vehicle* that transports your prayers or requests to God for God to deliver your fulfilled desires to you. If your mind does not drift to your undesired outcomes, then do you think you will need to grow your faith?

Me: No.

God: Exactly. One component of faith is **believing**. You do not have to believe something if you already **know** something. Knowing is the same as awareness. The only reason why you have to believe that God will do something for you is that you do not fully know that he has done it yet. In the physical realm, you only know something when you can experience it with your five senses. Until you can experience something with your five senses, you have to use *faith* to bring what you believe or see with your sixth sense into the awareness of your five senses. Every vehicle that man has made has to overcome friction. This is the reason why the efficiency of a machine is not always equal to 100 percent. Your vehicle of faith has to overcome friction too. If there is no undesired situation for your mind to drift to, your vehicle of faith will not be necessary.

So you see that your faith cannot exist without your possible undesired outcomes. This means that your possible undesired outcomes are very good. Your possible undesired outcomes give you an opportunity to experience the God that you really are. Therefore, do not consider the undesired outcomes that your mind keeps drifting to as bad or negative. Whenever your mind drifts to any undesired or negative outcome, do not reject it. Instead, gently acknowledge it, then gently switch your attention to what you desire, with the full assurance that the God you believe in is able to overcome the undesired outcomes. If you deny the negative outcomes, you will not have an opportunity to exercise your faith. This is because faith can only exist in the presence of an undesired outcome. Also, it is crucial to notice something very subtle, but extremely important here...

First, your mind has a steering wheel, just like a car. It is called focus or attention. You need to take hold of your focus or attention at all points in time in order to get you to where you want to go. When you take your hands off the steering wheel of your mind, by losing focus or attention on your desires or fulfilled prayers, your mind will sometimes drift to the things you do not desire. If your belief system is very strong or you have a high awareness of my Principles, then even when your mind drifts, it is highly likely that it will drift towards my Principles that are beneficial to you. This is another reason for you to seek my Principles.

Second, you cannot pray to receive something without considering for a brief moment, usually for a second or more, your undesired outcomes, or slightly less desirable outcomes, that your mind can drift to. In other words, you must either have some form of undesired outcome, or less desirable outcome that your mind can drift to, before you can pray to receive something.

Me: But wait. Considering all that you have been telling me about focusing on my fulfilled prayers, who in their right mind would think about their undesirable situation before they pray? You told me *not* to focus on my unde-sired conditions, and now, you are telling me to have an undesired condition in mind before I can pray? Isn't that contradictory?

God: No, it's not. Everyone does it subconsciously or unconsciously. If you don't believe me, then I suggest you try this simple experiment... The next time you pray for something or you thank me for something, quickly ask yourself this question: "What was going on in my mind before I prayed?" You will notice that prior to thanking me, you had a thought about what it felt like to not have what you are thanking me for. You will also notice that prior to your prayer, you had a brief thought about your undesired situation or possible outcomes. Because you are not always aware of this brief thought, you think that you do not focus on your undesired outcomes before you pray, but you do. This happens to all people. The key is to only consider your undesired outcomes or current circumstances for only a brief moment, usually for a few seconds. Then use the discomfort you get from your brief thought as a *springboard* to pray, by switching your attention to the feelings of having your prayers fulfilled. If you do this, you will eventually increase your prayers to the stage of passion.

On the other hand, if it's necessary for you to look at your undesired circumstances or outcomes a little longer for the purpose of developing or thinking about a solution, then that is fine. However, generally speaking, my suggestion to you is that you cultivate a habit of permanently having the feelings of your spiritually fulfilled prayers manifested, but a casual habit of mentally looking at your undesired circumstances or possible outcomes. This habit is the same as the refocusing of your attention on your spiritually fulfilled prayers each time your mind drifts to your undesired outcomes. **This habit is what gives you an opportunity to repeat your ordinary thought (lowest form of prayer), so that your ordinary thought can become a wish, then a desire, then a passion, and then the needed awareness.** When you notice that your mind has drifted to your undesired possible outcomes, you are not supposed to drift along with it. But instead, refocus your mind on your spiritually fulfilled prayers. It does not matter so much where your mind drifts to, but rather, what matters is where you redirect your attention upon noticing that your mind has drifted. If you keep your attention on your fulfilled prayers by your fervent imagining of your fulfilled prayers, you will not have to worry about where your mind drifts to. However, if your mind drifts, just refocus your mind on your fulfilled prayers, and know that the drifting of your mind to your undesired outcomes cannot harm you.

Also, if your mind does not drift to your undesired outcomes to prompt you to pray, you will probably only pray about your desires sporadically instead of persistently or fervently. You cannot pray about your desires once every month and expect quick answers. It must be daily, and if possible, hourly, and if possible, minute by minute, and if possible, second by second. This is an essential part of what it takes to produce an effective, fervent prayer that avails much. Therefore, the drifting of your mind is a huge opportunity, or a reminder, for you to accelerate the manifestation of your spiritually fulfilled prayers in the physical realm, through the refocusing of your attention.

Finally, the drifting of your mind is really me, at a lower vibration, asking you if you really meant what you said in your last prayer.

Me: Whaat?! I can't believe it! So you have been tricking me all this while?

God: No, I have not been tricking you. I have only been asking you whether you really mean what you say, or whether you are serious about getting what you have been praying for. Your job is to respond with a firm "yes" by refocusing your attention back on your fulfilled prayers with gratitude, rather than the negative outcomes your mind keeps drifting to. Notice again that I said your job is to refocus on your "fulfilled prayers" instead of your "prayers." To focus on your fulfilled prayers is to use your imagination to feel what it will be like to have your prayers answered in the physical realm. If you don't remember how to do this, then I will suggest you review the second faith accelerant we discussed in this book, which is "feeling." Once you say yes to me over and over, I will know that you really mean what you say and that you are passionate about it. Once you are passionate about something, I move at lightning speed to bring you the needed awareness to manifest what you are passionate about. You only need to pay attention to my promptings, my nudges, and the many other signs that I bring around you. Just make sure you don't call them "coincidences."

On the other hand, if you say "no" by focusing your attention on the undesired outcomes that your mind drifts to, then I will keep asking you the same or similar question over and over. I will do this until you either say "yes," or give up on your prayer. Once you give up on your prayer, you will ultimately start a new prayer, and the cycle will begin again.

An important note to keep in mind is that it is okay for your mind to drift. However, if you don't like what your mind drifts to, then it is *not* okay for you to focus on your undesired outcomes once you are conscious of the fact that your mind has drifted to an undesired outcome.

Me: Wow. That is very interesting and wonderful.

God: Also, the drifting of your mind to your undesired outcome is what ultimately produces joy upon the fulfillment of your prayers. This is so because you will ultimately end up comparing your physically fulfilled prayers with the possible undesired outcomes that your mind previously drifted to, in order to get a variance.

This variance is called "joy." Without this variance, joy will not exist. This joy is what produces a sense of accomplishment in life.

However, at a higher level of your spiritual understanding, or growth, or awareness, you will hardly need any variance between your desired and undesired outcomes in order to find joy, as you will have *become* joy. At this stage, you will hardly have a need to briefly consider your undesired outcomes as a springboard to increase your prayers to the level of passion. As your joy increases, your mind will drift less and less to your undesired outcomes. This is because you will have many beneficial Principles activated within you to the extent that your mind will have no place to drift to, but to my activated Principles that are beneficial.

Therefore, you will know how far you are growing in my Principles by how far away and how often your mind drifts to your undesired outcomes. When you *become* joy, you will amazingly find yourself being happy and grateful for the things in life that most people would call insignificant – such as the specks of dust in the air, time with family and friends, the rain, the wind, the skies, the stars, and literally everything. When you *become* joy, you will not be moved or be disturbed by even the biggest, seemingly insurmountable challenges of life. The drifting of your mind is what some people call "the influence of the devil," but it is actually a blessing in disguise.

Let me explain further why the drifting of your mind is a blessing. When you are truly in the present moment, and your mind has not drifted, your vibration is set to neutral. You are a vibrational being, and your normal vibrational state is neutral. Neutral simply means you are vibrating at your normal state. When your mind drifts to something you do not like, your vibration moves to the reverse state or a level below your normal state. It is only from the reverse state or the undesired place where your mind drifts to, that you can vibrate or move beyond your normal vibrational state to a forward position. The forward position is the place of your fulfilled prayers or desires.

This is the same as saying that in order for you to jump, you first have to bend your knees. If you do not bend your knees, it is impossible for you to jump. So your mind drifting to your undesired state is a fortune, and a blessing, as it gives you a point of reference to jump from.

The drifting of your mind can either be a fortune or a misfortune. It is a fortune if you see it as an opportunity to raise your desires to a passionate level, and subsequently to a higher level of awareness. And it is a misfortune when you drift along with your mind to your undesired possible outcomes. If you do not see the drifting of your mind as an opportunity to switch to your spiritually fulfilled prayers, then rather than getting your fortune, you will get the misfortune that comes with focusing on your undesired outcomes. Or, rather than moving forward in life, you will move backward in the fulfillment of your prayers.

Me: Wait, this sounds really good. This is almost like what is said in Neal Donald Walsh's book called "Conversations with God." It states that "...in the absence of that which you are not, that which you are is not."

God: Yes, this is true.

Me: Again, this sounds really good, but it is easier said than done.

God: It is *supposed* to be easier said than done. What do you think I did to create the universe? I simply spoke everything into existence because it was easier for me to speak than to do. It will also be easier for you to speak it than to do it. The way you speak it is to verbally and non-verbally speak about your spiritually fulfilled prayers frequently, by switching your mind's attention to the feelings of having your prayers fulfilled. After speaking about your spiritually fulfilled prayers to the point of passion, your body and mind will unconsciously end up doing the needed work for you, without you feeling exhausted.

Let me give you another analogy that will help you understand. Assume that there is a big fire outbreak on a small piece of farmland that you own. And let's also assume that you have lots of water and a water hose to quench the fire. What will you do when you first recognize that there is a fire outbreak? Will you deny that there is a fire outbreak, or will you just stand still and stare at the fire?

Me: No, I will acknowledge that there is a fire outbreak. However, I will also take my water hose and spray some water on the fire to quench it.

God: Exactly, this is the same way that faith works. Acknowledging that there is a fire outbreak is the same as gently acknowledging the negative outcomes that your mind keeps drifting to. If you don't acknowledge the fire, then you will ignore it, and the fire will burn the whole farm. You *gently* acknowledge the fire simply because you are not scared of the fire as you know that you have the solution, which is your water to quench the fire. As you go through the process of spraying the water on the fire, you know within your mind that it is just a matter of time before you finish spraying the water on all the fire. In fact, as you spray the water on the fire, you can actually see in your mind what the farm will look like after the fire is fully quenched.

This is the same thing that happens when you exercise your faith. Don't *disregard* all the negative things your mind drifts to. But rather, gently acknowledge them, and gently switch your attention to the desired outcome, which in this analogy is your water hose with water. The act of switching back and forth between the undesired outcome, which is fire, and the desired outcome, which is a farm without fire, is the act of exercising your faith. It is impossible for you to exercise your faith without you switching back and forth between the undesired outcomes and the desired outcomes. As I mentioned earlier in this chapter, you can intentionally use the discomfort you get from your undesired thoughts as a springboard to pray, think about solutions, or brainstorm. Other than that, you do not have to follow your mind every time it drifts away to your undesired outcomes. But even when you are brainstorming or thinking about solutions, whether you arrive at a satisfactory solution or not, make sure to end your thoughts by switching your mind to your desired outcomes by faith. Therefore, don't get over fixated and nervous about your undesired outcomes, but rather, switch your attention to your desired outcomes when your mind drifts away and smile even more.

Know that your faith must have some kind of friction to overcome. The undesired outcomes that your mind drifts to cannot harm you unless you unnecessarily *dwell* on them in your conscious mind. Over time, as you keep switching your mind to your desired outcomes, you will notice that your mind will become accustomed to drifting to your desired outcomes instead of your undesired outcomes. Also, remember that one component of faith is *action*, as we discussed earlier in this book. So as you keep switching back and forth between the undesired outcomes and the desired outcomes, make sure to also take actions that will propel you to the desired outcomes while believing in God. Remember that I am more than able to bring into physical existence what you desire. And I can perform exceedingly abundantly above what you can desire, think, or imagine. In some situations, when you have exhausted all that you can do, you will not have to do anything. Instead, you will only have to focus on your desired outcomes with thanksgiving.

Moreover, remember that the act of switching your mind from the undesired outcomes to your desired outcomes is what gives you a chance to apply my Principles. The drifting of your mind gives you an opportunity to exercise your faith, so that you can please me. For without faith, it is impossible to please God. I will always love you regardless of where your mind drifts to, or what you do. However, you cannot please me if you do not *make persistent, conscious* attempts to learn how to effectively and efficiently use my Word. For without my word, you cannot have faith. And without my Word, or my Principles, or my promises, you cannot effectively switch your mind from your undesired outcomes to your desired outcomes.

Me: Okay, but hold on. You just introduced the word "promises." Are your promises the same as your Principles?

God: Yes, they are, and I merely used the word "promise" here to get your attention. The truth is that I do not have any promises.

Me: Whaaat! So you mean you have been lying to me all this time?

God: No, I have been telling you the truth. Let me explain. I only used the word "promise" because most human beings, who do not understand who they are, like the word "promises." They take my promises on face value, and they do not seriously participate in either gaining understanding of my promises, nor partnering with me to execute my promises. Hence, they lack meaningful manifestations in their life. On the contrary, human beings who know who they are take time to study, understand, and execute my promises. Hence, they don't remind me of my promises to persuade me to do something for them.

The ultimate truth is that God does not need to promise you anything. Whenever you see a *promise* of God in the Bible, it is only telling you who God is. God is pure love, and love can never hurt itself. When I tell you that I promise to protect you, I am merely telling you that one of my attributes is **a protector**. I cannot promise you something that I am not. My attributes, or my nature, or who I am, is love, and out of my love flows protection, prosperity, good health, kindness, and all greater things that pertain to life and Godliness. To put it in a context that you can relate to, I will say that out of who I am, flows the fruits of the spirit, which are: love, joy, peace, forbearance, kindness, goodness, faithfulness, gentleness, and self-control – as stated in Galatians 5:22-23.

Once you know and understand my Word, you will not say: "Oh, God, remember that you promised me this and that...?" But rather, you will *become* my promise. This is the same as saying that once you are rich and have all the money you need, you will not have to ask me for money anymore. My promises are myself, my promises are my attributes, and my promises are what defines who I am.

Me: Are you saying there is something wrong with me reminding you of what you have promised me? Especially in the Bible?

God: Absolutely not. There is nothing wrong with you reminding me of my promises. However, I want you to understand that once you get to know me better, or once you grow up a little bit more spiritually, you will not even need to remind me of myself anymore because I cannot forget who I am. In other words, I cannot forget my promises in the same way you cannot forget that you have two legs and two hands. My promises are my Principles, and when you apply my Principles, you will definitely get the outcome that you desire without having to remind me of myself. However, until you have spiritually matured enough to not have to remind me of my promises, it is okay to keep reminding me of my promises. This is because the act of reminding me of my promises actually increases your faith and thereby makes it easy for you to access my goodness. Your reminders will not change me, but rather, they will change you by increasing your faith. Once your faith is increased, you can be assured of an acceleration in the manifestation of your prayers. This is another reason why I told you to listen to, read, or study my Word as a faith accelerant. For the sake of your understanding, I will use promises to refer to my Word as I speak to you. But keep in mind that my promises are my attributes, and I cannot change my attributes. I am the same yesterday, today, and forever more. *All my promises are Yes and Amen.* That means I am a faithful God. My promises make it easy for you to switch from your undesired thoughts to your desired thoughts. You do not have to know all my promises or Principles at once to be able to switch. For example, if you know that one of my promises is that you are more than a conqueror, and you believe it, then with that knowledge, you can easily switch to your desired outcome when your mind drifts. If you really understand what the mind is doing when it drifts, as I have explained here to you, it will become harder and harder for you to doubt my promises. If you understand what I just explained, you will be able to stand firm on my promises in all situations. And you will be able to experience miracles that you've only read about in the Bible, such as the miracle of Daniel in the lions' den, or the miracle of Shadrach, Meshach, and Abednego in the fire.

Me: Wow, that is really beautiful! Thank you. Thank you so much for that explanation.

God: There is one more thing that I need to mention here. Do you remember that I told you that *faith* is like a vehicle that transports your requests or prayers to me?

Me: Yes.

God: Now, also remember that I am a faithful God, and my promises are Yes and Amen. I am very faithful to myself, and I cannot deny myself. I have many names that describe who I am. Faithfulness is one of my names. In order for you to get a taste of my Faithfulness, you need a vehicle called faith. Your faith brings out my Faithfulness. My Faithfulness is essentially who I am. My Faithfulness is my awareness; it is all that I am made of. It is pure consciousness. My Faithfulness is my Principles. I am my Principles, and I am Faithfulness. The only way to see me is to come to me with faith. No vehicle can enter my house that is not called faith. Therefore, come to me with faith, and I will give you my Faithfulness, so that your faith will become Faithfulness. And then you will become as I am, and We will be One consciously, subconsciously, and Superconsciously. Out of your faith comes my

Faithfulness. The use of your faith will make you see me and become me. Once you become Faithfulness, many people will run to you by their faith, both physically and spiritually, to gain some of your Faithfulness, just as you first ran to me to get my Faithfulness. And the more you give out your Faithfulness, the more Faithfulness will come to you and the more Faithfulness you will become. Also, remember that the more you exercise your faith, the more your faith will increase. And the more your faith increases, the more and more you will become Faithfulness, which is still me. Finally, when you become Faithfulness, you will have completed the cycle of first starting with faith and then finishing with Faithfulness. And that makes you the author and the finisher of faith, which Jesus exemplified, as it is described in your Bible (Hebrews 12:2).

CHAPTER 5

SPIRITUAL ORDER-OF-OPERATION

As we noted earlier, most prayers are offered in order to get something from God. That something is either a cause or an effect. Causes and effects are the same, but you will be happier getting causes rather than effects, as causes have the capability of replicating effects over and over, and over again. Causes, as you know, are the same as my Principles or my Word. You also recall that my Word is myself, which is to say that the Word is God himself. Therefore, seek the Word, search for it with all your heart and mind, and all things, which are effects, will be added unto you.

Me: Wait a minute, I think I just got an idea. Tell me if I am correct. Is what you are talking about the same as the law of detachment or what is said in Buddhism that: "You only lose what you cling to" in the physical realm?

God: Absolutely. Boooy, you are certainly growing in

intuitive awareness! Good for you! This is the law of detachment at its core. It is more rewarding to be attached to the causes of life than to be attached to the effects of life. If you get too attached to the effects of life and obtain the effects of life, then you will be very miserable every time you lose the effects that you have. But if you get attached to the causes of life, you will never lose the effects, as the causes can always reproduce the effects. Jesus taught this, Saint Paul taught this, and many others have also taught this. This is what is meant by, "...seek first the kingdom of God and all things shall be added unto you" (Matthew 6:33). The kingdom of God is the Principles of God applied. It is the cause of life, it is the Word, it is life itself, and it is God. Once you have God, all things automatically become yours. This explains the richness of Solomon in the Bible, and this also explains why Jesus said that you are *in* this world, but not *of* this world. Jesus meant that you should be the cause of the things in this world, and not the effects, as the effects keep changing and would keep you trapped. But the causes are stable, and they will give you a stable and a peaceful life. In your spare time, look up the following Bible scriptures that explain being detached from the effects of this life and being attached to the Word: 1 Corinthians 1: 29-31 and Matthew 19:21. Also, remember to enjoy the process of finding the Principles, as the process itself is also life. The process is the Word, and the Word is God. Don't wait till you learn all the Principles before you enjoy life, as doing so will defeat the purpose. Be open-minded, enjoy every moment of life, and enjoy God at all times.

Me: What a beautiful explanation! I love it! I love it!

God: Okay, now that you know the importance of understanding my Principles, it is also important that you understand my spiritual order-of-operations. My order-of-operations are rules that govern the use of my Principles. The rules themselves are also Principles. So, there are Principles that govern other Principles. I will call the Principles that govern other Principles "rules," so that you don't get confused. I am going to explain two rules or order-of-operations that are extremely important. If you understand these two rules, you will be able to understand why some of your prayers get answered quickly, and why some do not. And you will consequently be able to utilize your understanding to speed up the manifestation of your prayers.

Rule 1 – Praying for Self: You cannot pray to get something that you are not. You cannot possess what you desire unless you know you are already what you desire. This rule means that in order for you to achieve anything, you first have to be an embodiment of the Principles that are capable of producing your desires. I will explain this in a little more detail for you in a few minutes.

Rule 2 – Praying for Others: You cannot give something to another person unless you already have it. And no one can receive something that they do not already have.

Let's say you are praying for someone, whom I will call the beneficiary, to get something. When you whole-heartedly or passionately pray for your beneficiary, you temporarily and automatically assume the awareness of the thing that you are praying for in the spiritual realm, even though that awareness may not be physically present in your life. Without first assuming the awareness, you cannot give it to another through prayer. If you temporarily assume a given awareness for the purpose of praying for another, then at some point in your life, this same temporary assumption or awareness will also present situations and circumstances for *you* to decide the extent to which you would like to physically manifest that given awareness. This does not mean that if the beneficiary was sick and you prayed for healing, then you would also get sick in order to manifest healing. But rather, you would become physically stronger or healthier in situations that you are not supposed to be. This is another reason why it is said that do unto others what you want others to do unto you.

Also, in order for the potential beneficiary of your prayer to receive the awareness that you are praying for, the potential beneficiary has to *assume* the awareness that you have prayed for. And the only way for this to happen is for the potential beneficiary to be capable of praying for himself or herself and others to receive the awareness that you prayed for.

Let me explain this with an example. Let's say John prays for Sarah to get a new car. Sarah can receive the manifestation of the new car if Sarah is capable of praying on a subconscious level for herself and all people to get a new car.

Me: What does it mean for Sarah to be capable of praying for herself and all people to get a new car on a subconscious level?

God: It does not mean Sarah has to pray for all people relative to what John has prayed about. Rather, this has two meanings. First, it means that Sarah must have a desire for a new car. And second, it means that Sarah must not harbor the thoughts of someone else not being able to achieve the same thing that John prayed for.

Me: Oh, okay.

God: Now, if Sarah is not capable of subconsciously praying for herself and all people to get a new car, and what John prayed for is something that will enhance the life of Sarah, then Sarah will be given an opportunity to have a thought about a new car in reference to herself and all people. This opportunity is part of my Grace and is granted by one's superconscious mind. Once Sarah subconsciously desires a new car, and she does not harbor the thoughts of someone else not being able to receive a new car, then she will get the opportunity to manifest a new car in her life as an answer to the prayer of John.

Me: Wait! Wait! I just got something. I have an idea. So, let's assume that Sarah does not have the praying capability you referenced above. And let's also assume that Sarah is going to get an opportunity by grace to pray or have thoughts about a new car relative to herself and others. Then, in this case, in addition to praying for Sarah, it will be great or expedient for John to take any acceptable action to help Sarah to understand on a conscious level that we are all one. Once Sarah understands this, Sarah will not want to have any ill-thoughts about another, as she will know that her ill-thoughts for another would be ill-thoughts for herself. This will make it easier for Sarah to pray for herself and to assume the having of a new car. By doing this, Sarah will not even need much grace to physically manifest a new car faster, as Sarah would have spiritually assumed the being or the having of a new car through the physical assistance that was offered by John.

God: Oh my God! How did you know that?!

Me: Wait a minute. Did you just call me God with a big "G"? I thought you are God.

God: Yes, I am, and you are too.

Me: What???

God: Before I tell you why I called you God, let me point out something to you.

Me: Okay.

God: How did you know that it would be easier for Sarah to manifest a new car if Sarah understands that all people are one?

Me: The idea just dropped in my head. Maybe, I just deduced it from what you said, or you gave me the thought.

God: You are saying that even though I am talking to you, and you are talking to me, you are also talking or hearing from another God?

Me: I don't really know.

God: I tell you that you just demonstrated an intuitive awareness that we just talked about. This is a perfect example of an intuitive awareness. Notice that you heard from a different voice other than the voice I am currently using. God has many voices. He can talk to you from many different angles, but once you become more aware of intuitive awareness, you will know that all voices are God's voice. Your job is to distinguish *all* the voices that you hear, and select the voice that inspires you the most to achieve your desires or prayers.

Me: But why does God have multiple voices? Why can't God just speak to me in one voice so that I can hear him easily?

God: Why do you eat different types of food every day? Doesn't it get boring when you eat the same thing all the time? God gets bored with the same voice too. God switches his voice and speaks to you through your family members, your pastors, your friends, your experiences, and in many other ways, but it is all one voice. It's all part of the fun – just enjoy it. As you become more aware, I promise that all the voices will merge into one voice, yet they will also be easily distinguishable, and you will know that all the voices are my voice.

Me: Okay, but it looks like you changed the subject on me. Could you tell me why you called me God? Even the Bible does not call humans God. The closest the Bible gets to on this subject is the fact that we are gods with a small letter "g." I have been told that we are smaller gods and that you are the big God with a big letter "G."

God: That is interesting. What do you think is the difference between a God with a big "G" and a god with a small "g"?

Me: The God with the big "G" created the universe and created the smaller gods. The God with the big "G" can do big things, and the god with the small "g" can do things that are a little smaller than what the God with the big "G" can do.

God: Okay. Now, do you believe that Jesus is God with a big "G?"

Me: Yes, I do. The Bible says that Jesus and God are one. It also says, in Philippians 2:6, that even though Jesus is God, he did not think of equality with God as something to be used for his own advantage. So yes, Jesus is God.

God: Okay, and does the Bible also say that the things that Jesus did, you and everyone else can do the same and even greater?

Me: Yes.

God: So if you are saying that you can do greater things than Jesus, yet Jesus is a big God, and you think you are a smaller god, then why do you say that small gods do smaller things, and God with a big "G" does big things

– when you are also admitting that you can do greater things than Jesus?

Me: Wait. You just confused me. What are you saying? If I can do greater things than Jesus, then why haven't I been able to walk on water yet, as Jesus did?

God: I tell you what, you should not have to necessarily desire to walk on water, but to fly over water, or walk on air, because you can certainly do greater things than Jesus did. All it takes is spiritual growth through daily spiritual practice, and that is exactly what you are doing now. The love that God has for Jesus is not different from the love that God has for you or anyone else. It is the same love. If God loves you and Jesus equally, then what makes you think you cannot do the same as Jesus did, or even better? And if you call Jesus God, and you believe that you can do better than Jesus, then why do you call yourself "god" with a small "g," and call Jesus "God" with a big "G"? I tell you what, you and Jesus and everyone else are all one, and I love you all equally. It is my deepest desire that you know this truth. Once you know this truth, then you can use me, use my Principles, use my Word, and use my wisdom, so that I can be God with a big "G" through you.

Me: Are you saying that you will not be God with a big "G" if I don't use your Word?

God: Even though we are one, if you don't use my Word, you will not know the God that you are. And this will make the God that you are dormant, and you will become a small god with a small "g," which in fact, is just an illusion of your mind. It is, therefore, the recognition and the using of my Word, or my Principles, that makes me God. And it is also the recognition and the using of my Principles that will make *you* God. It is not you calling yourself God that makes you God, but the use of my Principles. Boast, therefore, not to be God, but use my Principles, and you will not only be God, with a big "G," but you will also be seen as God with a big "G" by many.

Me: Oh, wow!! What an explanation!! I have to think about this a little deeper to come to terms with it. But thank you.

God: You are welcome! We got sidetracked for a minute, but let's return to our conversation about Rule 2. The second part of Rule 2 states that you cannot receive something that you do not already have. This also means that you cannot pray for someone to do something for you unless you are the thing that you are praying for. This second part directly ties in with Rule 1, which states that you cannot pray to get something that you are not, so let me give you an example that will explain both Rule 1 and the second part of Rule 2.

Let's say you need a favor from your boss for something. In applying this rule, you have to ask yourself: What if you were in your boss's situation? Would you do for another what you want your boss to do for you? If your answer is no, then go out and do for another, the same or similar favor you want your boss to do for you. Even if your answer is *yes*, by going out and doing a similar favor for another, you will increase the speed with which you will receive a favor that is the same as, or similar to, the favor you need. And you will also be increasing how often, or the frequency, with which someone will honor your desires. Make sure, however, that you genuinely *want* to do things for others, rather than wanting to trick the universe, because the universe knows your true feelings and true reasons for doing something. Once you know that you and all other people are one, you will find it easier and more joyful to help others. This is one of the primary teachings of Jesus. Jesus taught that what you do to another, you do to him, and what you do to him, you do to another. Therefore, when you pray for anything that requires another person to do something for you, make sure that you have the right standing to receive what you pray for.

A final example is that when you pray to God for God to ask someone who owes you to come and pay you, ask yourself this question: "Do I owe someone that I have not paid?" If you owe someone that you have not paid, then make an effort to call the person and either pay the person or make a genuine arrangement to pay the person. In so doing, not only will you obtain the right standing to receive what you pray for, but you will also obtain the right standing to receive it sooner than later.

Me: Wow! That is amazing! So essentially, when you cheat someone, you cheat yourself by placing yourself in the wrong standing for God to answer your prayers.

God: Yes, but also remember that to be in good standing is the same as being *righteous*. This is my Principle, and I will ensure that the righteous do not ever go hungry.

CONCLUSION

God: Now you have the basic, yet the advanced knowledge or techniques to bring what is happening in Heaven to Earth. Go now and let all the world know of me. Let them know that they can all talk to me through prayers: through their ordinary thoughts, through their wishes, through their desires, and through their passion. And I will be right there to give myself to them. I will be right there to give them my Principles, or my Word, or my Truths, or my Promises, or my Faithfulness, or my Awareness, or my Ways, or Myself, and how to use Me. Know that I love you, and remember that you are my only begotten son, in the form that you are made, in whom I am well pleased. You are more than a conqueror. Be cheerful, and enjoy my unchanging, eternal Principles of prayer.

Me: Thank you.

God: Now go and get some sleep.

Me: Wait! Wait! Wait! Don't leave me yet. We've got more books to write.

God: Don't worry, I will never leave you nor forsake you. We are inseparable just as I am inseparable from everybody and everything else.

Me: Okay, okay, okay. Good night, God.

God: Oh, now, that sounds rather like you are trying to leave me. I thought we are supposed to be together at all times with me living in you and you living in me. When you said "Good night," it sounded like you were trying to leave me while you go to sleep for the night, and that you will see me in the morning. Rather than saying "Good night," let's say, "Good life" to all of us, as we are joined together for eternity.

Me: That really, really, sounds better, but I think I have a much better way to say it.

God: Tell me about it.

Me: Magnificent life to Us.

God: That definitely sounds better. Magnificent life, my love, my friend, my son, my brother, and my partner.

Me: Wait, one more thing. Can I give you a kiss?

God: Yes, you can. Every time you kiss your spouse, children, family, or friends, you will be giving me a kiss.

Me: Yes, I know, but I don't mean it like that. I want to give you a kiss. I understand all the esoteric and spiritual reasons that we are one, but I mean, I want to give you an actual kiss that I can feel.

God: My son, I know what you mean, but I tell you that when you kiss another person, you are really, really kissing me, because I am in all people. It is not just some esoteric theory or spiritual thing, but it is really practical and real. It is more practical than you can think.

Me: Okay, fine, if you say so.

God: Well, just to satisfy your request, go ahead and give me a kiss with your imagination.

Me: Alright. Are you ready?

God: Don't ask me if I am ready. Just do it.

Me: Okay; mmmmmmmmmmmmwaaah!

God: Mmmmmmmmmmmmmmmmmmwaaaaaah!

Me: Magnificent life to Us.

God: Magnificent life to Us.

MESSAGE FROM THE AUTHOR

First, I just want to say thank you, thank you, and thank you for reading this book. I hope you have been blessed. Thank you again.

Second, I would love to get your feedback on how this book has impacted you. So, would you please spend one or two minutes to write a candid review about your impressions on this book on Goodreads or where ever you purchased your copy. Feel free to share any impressions (e.g.: How has this book benefited you? Did you get your money's worth? Would you recommend this book? Etc.) Your effort would be greatly appreciated.

Third, many readers have asked me when my next conversation with God will be released. If you are interested in being notified of the release date, or if you simply want to connect with me, then please feel free to follow me on Amazon.com to get future updates on my upcoming books.

Finally, I'd love to hear from you, so don't hesitate to contact me if you have any questions or feedback, or if you simply need some additional resources. My contact information is as follows:

Website: www.callgodphone.com
Email: danielpublishing@yahoo.com

With gratitude,

Daniel Essien